THE TIMES
PICTURE COLLECTION
LONDON

THE TIMES
PICTURE COLLECTION
LONDON

Ian Harrison

TED SMART

Foreword

THIS BOOK IS NOT A HISTORY of London, nor a glossy compilation of familiar 'sights'. The world hardly needs another one of those. Rather, it reveals a great city through the eyes of a great newspaper.

Despite the impression we may sometimes give, journalists are not entirely devoid of reflective or visionary thoughts. But the meat and drink of any daily newspaper is the 'here and now', and *The Times* has been reporting the 'here and now' of London for more than two hundred years. This book dips into its incomparable archives to present photographs of London that stretch back to the early years of the 20th century.

All capture 'here and now' moments: unique, unrepeatable. Snapped by photographers racing to meet that night's deadline, they would have been published within 24 hours, and wrapping fish and chips within 48. This is the transient essence of the inky trade called journalism.

But it is also the essence of London. Though it has been around for 2,000 years, the city has never lost its restless, bustling, impermanent air. London life is not a single stream, but the confluence of a million events. And the 'spirit of London' is not only found in its grand buildings or tranquil parks, but in the multitudinous activities of its teeming populace; not only in its pomp but also in its circumstance; not only in its timeless routines but also in its limitless capacity to shock, amuse, delight, inspire and – occasionally – horrify.

Some images here, particularly the extraordinarily powerful photographs of the Blitz and riot-torn Brixton, recall eras of immense civic trauma. Others, such as the spectacle of a homeless man searching a litter bin for food on Christmas Day in the supposedly 'affluent' 1990s, attest to a civic shame that seems to leave a blacker stain on each passing decade.

Other images capture moments when the sublime gave way to the delightfully surreal. Most Londoners have gazed up in awe at the Whispering Gallery of St Paul's; few have witnessed a parachutist jump from it – and, miraculously, live to tell the tale. Many have seen Tower Bridge open; few have seen it open for a floating three-bedroomed house. Many have seen Old Masters in the National Gallery; few have seen them casually carried up the escalators at Piccadilly Circus.

Nobody 'knows' London. Not the whole of it. Even its finest chroniclers – Dickens, Pepys, Eliot – offer but a glimpse of one epoch, one story. London has a million stories running at once. Dark secrets lurk behind elegant façades; the bizarre lies just beyond the bland; and we chart our own passing years by the bewildering speed at which the city changes. Are you old enough to remember Dockland when it had docks? The Floral Hall when it had flowers? Fleet Street when it had newspapers?

Like the Thames, the mighty city never stands still. It can only be captured in snapshots. But on these pages it has been captured by some of the best snappers in the business.

Richard Morrison
The Times

Contents

Introduction

Ian Harrison

THE TIMES HAS BEEN RECORDING EVENTS from around the world, in Britain generally and in London in particular, for more than two centuries, since it was founded as the *Daily Universal Register* in 1785. In that time *The Times* introduced many journalistic firsts that we now take for granted, including the use of foreign correspondents, editorial independence from government – and the use of illustrations. Newspaper illustrations now take the form of photographs, and *The Times* has an extensive library of photographic archives stored in a network of brick-vaulted former wine cellars beneath the site of the warehouses that once lined the London Docks in Wapping. Photography did not exist when those warehouses were completed in 1805 but today the wine cellars that outlived them are filled with tens of thousands of images taken throughout the last century to illustrate the news of the day.

The art of photography has come a long way since the pioneering experiments of Thomas Wedgwood (son of the potter), Louis Daguerre and Fox Talbot. Techniques have changed enormously, and the archives of *The Times* Picture Collection range from glass plates dating from the early days of photography to electronic images captured on digital cameras at the turn of the millennium.

The photographs chosen from *The Times* Picture Collection for this look at London range from the quirky to the mundane, from national events to the minutiae of everyday life, from the F.A. Cup Final to Sunday morning football. They illustrate the tranquillity of parks and temples and the roar of rush-hour traffic, the grand hotels and the shelters for the homeless, the destructive results of terrorist bombs and the adventurous new architecture rising on the London skyline. Some of these photographs were taken to record significant events for posterity while others were just passing moments, forgotten with the weather report and the crossword; some were artfully composed, others snapped on the spur of the moment; some capture parks and buildings that are part of the heritage of the city (and the nation), others show moments from the lives of ordinary Londoners. And while many of the images were chosen because they are excellent photographs in their own right, others were selected because of their subject matter rather than their photographic merit. That is where this book differs from other collections of London views: the photographs are not the work of one artist, nor were they taken to illustrate the city at its most beautiful, most historic, most colourful, or most successful. They are press photographs, taken by an enormous team of staff and freelance photographers over a 90-year period and, because of that, they provide not a unified tour of London seen through the lens of one expert viewer but a gritty kaleidoscope of images, more lively and more down-to-earth than the usual collection, and not shying away from sometimes depicting the ugly side of life in the capital.

The Times Picture Collection is rich in images of London, partly because the paper is London-based and partly because so many events of national interest take place in the capital. As the seat of government, the home of the royal family, the financial engine of the country and the centre of media and fashion, London is news. And yet most of the pictures that appear in this book are not of news events as such, they show ordinary Londoners going about their daily lives: commuters streaming across London Bridge, traffic at the Elephant and Castle, people relaxing in London's parks, workmen cleaning Big Ben. Given their location, each one of these mundane events takes place against a fascinating historical backdrop: the first London Bridge was built by the Romans, a later one was pulled down by a Norwegian king, and the last one was bought by an American and now stands in the Arizona desert; the original Elephant and Castle tavern was used by archers from Newington Butts long before the traffic arrived (a butt is a mound or mark used for archery practice); most of London's royal parkland was taken from the church by Henry VIII for use as hunting grounds, and the workmen are cleaning not just a clock but a symbol of British democracy whose chime is broadcast around the world – Big Ben.

But how to make sense of this wealth of images, showing so many different aspects of London life? The answer was to group them together very loosely by theme. Most of the photographs in the 10 chapters were easy to classify (*London's River, Multicultural London, London at War, London – the Bleaker Side*) but many of them could have appeared in any one of several chapters: for example, the workmen cleaning Big Ben could have been classified as Londoners at work, as a London landmark or as a London icon; Clapham Common and Hackney Marshes could have come under

Green London or *London at Play*. The chapter headings are therefore a guide, to put the myriad images of the city into some sort of perspective and to make sure that the green spaces and the lives of Londoners themselves, at work and at play, are as prominent as the oft-pictured landmarks, the bricks and mortar of the city. And though they all have London in common, the images that make up *The Times Picture Collection: London* are not intended to provide a comprehensive history of a modern city or a compendium of the capital's news stories during the 20th century – they were chosen simply because they had something to say about life in one of Europe's most vibrant cities, whether through an unusual view of a familiar sight or through a striking image of an everyday event.

The first chapter, *London Landmarks*, is a selection of some of the capital's familiar sights in an unfamiliar light: most people would recognise Trafalgar Square, but very few have seen it from Nelson's point of view; many visitors have seen the chimneys of Battersea Power Station on the skyline but not its cavernous interior, and certainly not when occupied by a string quartet in hard hats serenading Margaret Thatcher. *London Icons* features a selection of photographs of people, places or objects that instantly say 'London': Chelsea Pensioners, the black cab, the London bus, Big Ben, Pearly Kings and Queens. Like most major cities London has its *Bleaker Side* and this, too, is part of the story, particularly when told through a newspaper archive where, sadly, bleak equals news. The story of London would not be complete without reference to the homelessness, street drinking, and prostitution that is happening within yards of monuments to London's success and affluence; it would be a distorted view of London's ethnic diversity not to refer to the riots at Brixton and Broadwater Farm, and it would be ignoring one of the most vexed political questions of the 20th century to pretend that the IRA had not affected life in London with its bombing campaign. The other chapter titles are self-explanatory, with the possible exception of *London Oddities*, a delightful collection of images of the quirky, hidden or downright odd side of London life. Here you will find football-playing nuns, a giant spider, a floating cricket pitch, a family living in a pepper pot and the lion that said hello each morning to Emile Zola – and you will also discover that at an international conference in 1884 London officially became the centre of the world.

A picture may be worth a thousand words but it cannot digress, go off at a tangent, make unexpected connections or reveal the background to what it shows. Throughout the book the text accompanying the photographs delves into the stories behind the images, often unearthing surprising gems such as where the brothers Cadbury got the idea for milk chocolate, which hotel milked a goat each morning for Mahatma Gandhi, where Emperor Haile Selassie stayed when he was in London, the fact that Christopher Wren designed pubs as well as churches, and that for 20 years the F.A. Cup Final was played at the Oval. The text also reveals that many of London's landmarks are known by the wrong names, including the NatWest Tower, Canary Wharf, Big Ben, Constitution Arch, and Eros; and that Chelsea FC is not in Chelsea, Kensington Gardens are not in Kensington, and the Angel, Islington, is not in Islington.

During the 18th century Dr Johnson told his biographer James Boswell that 'I think the full tide of human existence is at Charing Cross', which is probably truer today than it was 200 years ago. The full tide of human existence may not actually congregate at Charing Cross but the site of the original cross is the designated centre of the most ethnically diverse city in the world, where some 200 languages are spoken and representatives of almost every part of the globe have chosen to live. Nineteenth-century Prime Minister Benjamin Disraeli described London as 'a nation, not a city' and, looking at the scope of these photographs, it is easy to see what he meant. Apart from the make-up of its population, London has not only the physical trappings of a city (the railway stations, cafés, factories, parks, offices, theatres, markets, etc.) but also the landmarks of a nation: the Houses of Parliament, St Paul's Cathedral, Wembley Stadium, the National Gallery, the British Museum.

London is a city that has inspired poets, painters, film-makers and writers but for all that it is the day-to-day lives of its inhabitants that make the city what it is, lives recorded and photographed by newspapers such as *The Times*. The overall picture of London that emerges from this diverse collection of photographs is not a panorama but a collage, in which the individual elements, disparate fragments of the whole, build up into a comprehensive portrait of the city; where a slight shift in perspective turns each separate photograph into a single pixel of a larger picture. Boswell wrote that '[I] often amused myself with thinking how different a place London is to different people': this book gives the reader the chance to see both perspectives, the different Londons of different people becoming a wide-ranging view of the city as a whole. *The Times Picture Collection: London* is a fascinating, multi-faceted portrait of a fascinating, multi-faceted city.

London
Land

marks

LONDON'S LANDMARKS WERE ALREADY SHAPING and defining the capital by the time William the Conqueror built the Tower of London just outside the city walls more than nine and a half centuries ago. Long before that the hill, now known as Tower Hill, was a significant enough landmark to give the city its Celtic name – Llyn-dun, the Hill by the Pool (the Pool being the natural harbour of the Pool of London, now divided by Tower Bridge).

Landmarks committed to canvas by Canaletto and Hogarth now stand alongside newcomers to a skyline that makes up the familiar backdrop for films such as *Lock, Stock & Two Smoking Barrels*, *Secrets and Lies*, *Sliding Doors*, and *Notting Hill*. From the Tower of London to Canada Tower (more popularly known as Canary Wharf) and from the dome of St Paul's, rising out of the ashes of the Great Fire of 1666, to the Millennium Dome, rising out of the confused politics of the late 20th century, London's landmarks have attracted admiration, ridicule, controversy and pride in almost equal measure.

The feelings evoked by London's monuments and architecture bring out the poet in people: a 'sorry meniscus' (social commentator Iain Sinclair on the Millennium Dome); 'Earth has not anything to show more fair' (Wordsworth on the view from Westminster Bridge); 'I think it's one of Richard's' (Norman Foster dismissing a riverside development by Richard Rogers); 'an outcrop of the genius of London itself' (David Sylvester on Battersea Power Station); 'a monstrous carbuncle on the face of a much-loved and elegant friend' (Prince Charles on a proposed design for the extension to the National Gallery).

Trafalgar Square stands at the centre of London and was once considered to be the heart of the British Empire. The square was laid out by Sir Charles Barry, architect of the Houses of Parliament, to commemorate Nelson's great victory, although for most visitors feeding the pigeons and making the most of the cooling water of the fountains is more important than any distant naval triumph.

As one of London's largest public squares, Trafalgar Square is a favourite spot for New Year's Eve celebrations and has, almost since its completion, been the focus for political demonstrations: the Chartists assembled here in 1848 for their march to Kennington Common and, more recently, the square has played host to demonstrations against nuclear weapons, apartheid and the poll tax. In May 1998 three Greenpeace protestors climbed Nelson's Column to demonstrate against Canada's destruction of its rainforest – the unfurling of the huge banner was carefully timed so that it appeared in the background of all the press photographs of the Queen arriving at Canada House for a meeting with Canadian Prime Minister Jean Chrétien.

above
Tourists cool off in the
fountains of Trafalgar
Square.
21st July 1990.

left
Reg Docel and his
daughter Lisa surprise
Lord Nelson on the 150th
anniversary of the
raising of the statue to
the top of the column.
21st October 1993.

above
Charing Cross Station
and Hotel, seen soon
after the South Eastern
Railway Company was
incorporated into the
Southern Railway.
(Not dated.)

Trafalgar Square emerged out of architect John Nash's Charing Cross Improvement Scheme of the early 19th century, although Nash did not live to see the creation of the square itself. Pre-dating the square, and now isolated on a small traffic island to the south of Nelson's column, is an equestrian statue of Charles I that stands on the site of the original Charing Cross, which was the last of 12 crosses erected in 1290 by Edward I to mark the places where his wife Queen Eleanor's funeral cortège rested on its way from Nottinghamshire to Westminster Abbey.

The cross was pulled down on the orders of Parliament in 1647 during the Civil War but a replica was built on the forecourt of Charing Cross Station by the South Eastern Railway Company in 1863 when the station and the hotel were built. The Charing Cross Hotel, seen here before and after its 1980s' makeover, was built in 1863–4 by E.M. Barry above Charing Cross Station. With 218 bedrooms, the hotel was one of the first buildings in the capital to be faced with artificial stone, and Sir John Betjeman considered the opulent dining room to be 'the most finely appointed in London'.

The station itself was designed by John Hawkshaw and opened in 1864 on the site of the old Hungerford Market, where Charles Dickens was employed as a boy filling jars with boot polish. Twenty-

four years after the station opened, Dickens' son helpfully pointed out that: 'It is worth bearing in mind that trains for Dover and elsewhere, starting from Charing Cross, reverse themselves on leaving Cannon-st, so that those who leave the former station with their backs to the engine will have to travel the rest of the way with their faces to it, and vice-versa.'

The station was celebrated for its lofty single-arch roof, but this grand architectural statement sadly collapsed during maintenance in 1905, killing six men and destroying the Avenue Theatre next door, since rebuilt and now known as the Playhouse. The replacement roof was later demolished to make way for Terry Farrell's Embankment Place, an office complex built over the platforms at the same time as the restoration of the hotel façade and completed in 1990. The huge arched profile of Embankment Place is inspired by the architecture of the typical Victorian trainshed – it has been acclaimed as one of London's most spectacular modern buildings but also derided as looking like an enormous jukebox on the north bank of the Thames.

Although Charing Cross has only six platforms it handles a large amount of rail traffic, and at the time of the later picture it was London's fourth busiest terminus.

opposite

'Eros', perhaps bored of standing on one foot watching the traffic, hitches a lift to the cleaners.
31st March 1953.

below

It all started with Bovril and Schweppes – the names may have changed but the neon remains as imposing as ever. Note the birthday greeting above the Coke advertisement.
15th October 1993.

Piccadilly Circus is most famous for two things – for the illuminations, still impressive despite the proliferation of neon elsewhere, and for 'Eros', probably the most frequently misnamed statue in the world.

The illuminations are striking for the way that they cling so closely to the buildings, recreating the curved frontage while completely obliterating the original, and because they are so densely crammed into one corner of this oddly-shaped junction. And the story of why the 'circus' is such an odd shape is also the story behind the lights.

At one time Piccadilly Circus was just that – a circular interchange, or circus, at the end of Piccadilly. It was formed in 1819 by the intersection of Piccadilly with John Nash's new Regent Street, and would have formed a crossroads except that the buildings surrounding the new junction had concave curved frontages similar to those around the present Oxford Circus. But this neat arrangement was destroyed in the 1880s by the formation of Shaftesbury Avenue, a new thoroughfare whose construction entailed demolishing the north-eastern quadrant of Piccadilly Circus and cutting a swathe through the slums to the north, dividing what is now Chinatown from the rest of Soho.

The demolition of part of Piccadilly Circus meant that the buildings previously hidden away to the north now faced directly onto the road junction, presenting their owners with lucrative advertising space. They quickly took advantage of the new technology of flashing, electrically lit advertisements by erecting large signs on their roofs, but the London County Council were successful in having them removed. However, there was nothing the LCC could do to prevent signs being attached to the façades

of the buildings, and by 1910 Bovril and Schweppes had paved the way for the brightly coloured illuminations that have been a feature of Piccadilly Circus ever since.

The reason that these famous signs are crammed into one corner of Piccadilly Circus and did not spread round the entire junction is that the freehold for the buildings facing the original circus is owned by the Crown Estate, whose leases were carefully drafted to allow veto over any proposed signs.

Just off-centre of this lop-sided junction is the famous Statue of Eros – except that it is not a statue, and it is not of Eros. Officially known as the Shaftesbury Memorial Fountain (subtly different in status from a statue), the figure actually represents not Eros, the God of Love, but the Angel of Christian Charity. This makes sense for a memorial to a great philanthropist (the 7th Earl of Shaftesbury) but the sculptor himself, Sir Alfred Gilbert, created some confusion by saying that the angel represented 'the blindfolded love sending forth… his missile of kindness', and the memorial became known as Eros almost immediately after it was unveiled in 1893.

The memorial fountain was moved to Embankment Gardens in 1922, while Piccadilly Circus underground station was excavated, and was returned in 1931, only to be moved to Egham eight years later for the duration of the Second World War. 'Eros' has also been removed several times for cleaning, as seen here in 1953 .

One thing that Gilbert never made clear was whether or not the figure was intended to be a sculptural pun on Shaftesbury's name: there is no arrow, or shaft, in the angel's bow, which is pointing at the ground – is the shaft buried?

below
Cleaning the horses of
the Wellington Arch as
they charge past Apsley
House towards
St George's Hospital,
which was founded at
Hyde Park Corner in 1733
so that the patients
could benefit from the
country air.
27th June 1964.

At the other end of Piccadilly (named after the ruffs, or pickadills, worn by the dandies who used to promenade there in the 17th century) stands another memorial with an identity crisis – Constitution Arch, originally known as the Wellington Arch and later as the Green Park Arch. It has recently undergone extensive renovation by English Heritage who have added to the confusion by listing it in their handbook as… the Wellington Arch!

As its original and most recent name suggests, the arch is a memorial to the Duke of Wellington. It was designed by the 25-year-old Decimus Burton as one of a pair of gateways: one, Burton's Hyde Park Screen, leading into Hyde Park, and the other forming an outer entrance into the grounds of Buckingham Palace via Constitution Hill. The second arch was erected in 1828 and it was subsequently decided that it should form the base of a monument to the Iron Duke, so in 1846 the arch was surmounted by a colossal bronze statue of the duke on his horse at Waterloo. This equestrian statue stood 28 feet high and weighed 40 tons, out of all proportion to the arch itself, and provoked much ridicule, including a cartoon in *Punch*.

The arch originally stood closer to Hyde Park than it does now but in 1882–83 it was dismantled and moved as part of a traffic management programme – even in the 19th century Hyde Park Corner was

considered such a bottleneck that a road-widening scheme was needed. The arch was moved the few yards to where it now stands and at the same time the over-sized statue of Wellington was removed to Aldershot, the home of the army. Apsley House, past which the horses are charging in this photograph, is the Duke of Wellington's London residence (the current duke still lives there), and has perhaps the most famous address in the capital: No1, London.

The statue that now surmounts the Wellington Arch was presented to the nation in 1912 by Lord Michelham in memory of his friend Edward VII, and represents *The Angel of Peace descending on the Chariot of War*. Ironically it was erected in 1914, just in time for the beginning of the First World War. The bronze group is by Adrian Jones, a former veterinary officer in the 3rd Hussars, who held a dinner for eight of his friends inside the huge sculpture shortly before its completion.

above
David Wynne's *Girl With a Dolphin*, sculpted in 1973, seen here on an icy winter night. It is the sister-piece to his *Boy With a Dolphin* (1975) on Cheyne Walk opposite Albert Bridge.
26th February 1991.

right
Ravenmaster David Cope with Hugine, one of two new ravens at the Tower of London.
7th June 1995.

David Wynne would have had problems providing even a snack for his friends inside his *Girl with a Dolphin*, which graces the forecourt of the Thistle Tower Hotel, close to Tower Bridge.

Although it is only just over one hundred years old, Tower Bridge is, with the possible exception of Big Ben, London's most famous landmark. It is so closely identified with the capital that it is often confused (in name, not profile) with London Bridge – it is said that the owners of an American theme park, who bought London Bridge and reassembled it in Lake Havasu City, Arizona, thought that they were buying Tower Bridge and only discovered their mistake when they unpacked the crates.

Tower Bridge was a triumph of Victorian engineering, created by engineer John Wolfe-Barry with architect Sir Horace Jones, who designed the bridge to be in architectural harmony with its ancient namesake the Tower of London. It opened on 30th June 1894, and has a stone-clad steel frame to support the enormous weight of the lifting arms of the roadway, known as bascules after the French for see-saw; bascule itself comes from two older French words, *battre*, meaning to bump or beat, and *cul*, meaning backside.

The Tower itself is officially a royal palace, although it is far better known in the popular imagination as a prison; indeed, one American author commented that 'the Tower of London is to poisoning, hanging, beheading, regicide, and torture what the Yankee stadium is to baseball'. The Tower's first prisoner was Ralf Flambard, Bishop of Durham, who was also one of the few to escape, lowering a rope from a window after getting the guards drunk. The last was Rudolf Hess, in 1941, although new evidence suggests that the man who then spent the rest of his life in Spandau jail was an impostor and not the real Hess.

As well as a prison, the Tower has also served as an observatory, an armoury, a mint, and, before the word 'zoo' was coined, a menagerie. The only remaining animals are the famous ravens, who are cared for by the Ravenmaster and his assistants, and have their wings clipped to guard against a prophecy that if they leave the Tower the monarchy will fall.

above

Lasers in front of
St Paul's Cathedral mark
the path of the proposed
Millennium Bridge four
years before it was first
opened.
10th December 1996.

opposite

A parachutist leaps
120 feet into the nave
of St Paul's from the
Whispering Gallery.
Daredevil or idiot,
depending on your point
of view.
October 1990.

The only new bridge to have opened in London since Tower Bridge is Norman Foster's 'blade of light', the wobbly Millennium Bridge which opened in 2000 but was almost immediately closed again. The lasers in this photograph of St Paul's, taken in December 1996, mark the path of the proposed bridge in a literal version of Lord Foster's metaphor.

Charles Dickens described St Paul's Cathedral as 'the most conspicuous building in London' and, despite the encroaching office buildings that have since diminished its scale, it is still an awesome presence. The building of this great cathedral spanned the reigns of four monarchs but only one architect, Sir Christopher Wren. Towards the end of its construction Wren was hauled up to the dome in a basket to supervise the work; by the time the cathedral was completed he was too old and frail to lay the last stone so his son performed the task on his behalf.

Biographer Jenny Uglow writes that a glimpse of the cathedral dome is 'like being hit across the eyes. It's like a Hogarth print, where all the buildings crush together, and all London's history, change, and hope amid squalor are caught in a monochrome flash'. St Paul's not only provides 'hope among squalor' but also became a symbol of hope and defiance for Londoners during the Blitz.

In 1990 a man whom police believed to be a member of the Dangerous Sports Club jumped 120 feet from the Whispering Gallery into the nave of the cathedral in what appeared to be a suicide leap until the green silk of his parachute billowed open just beneath the parapet. Several hundred tourists and churchgoers looked on in astonishment as he crashed into the chairs in the nave below, knocking over a woman as he did so, and then disentangled himself from his parachute and fled on foot. A cathedral spokesman described the stunt as 'stupid, dangerous and highly irresponsible' – which is probably why he did it in the first place.

If the 17th-century church authorities had had their way there would have been no Whispering Gallery for the parachutist on the previous page to jump from – the bishops felt that a dome was unsuitable for an English cathedral and would have preferred a spire. With hindsight it is easy to see that Wren created a masterpiece of architecture, but at the time his dome was as controversial as Richard Rogers' Millennium Dome more than three hundred years later.

Whereas St Paul's rose out of the ashes of the Great Fire of London, the Millennium Dome rose out of wasteland contaminated by one of Europe's largest gasworks on what was once Bugsby Marshes. The site is seen here with the twelve 295-foot masts in place, its symmetry marred by the ventilation shaft of the Blackwall Tunnel that runs beneath. The circle is over half a mile in diameter and when the fabric was hung on these giant tent poles it was more than 165 feet high at its centre, making the Dome by far the world's largest. The 'skin' of the Dome, Iain Sinclair's 'sorry meniscus', was originally to have been PVC but a successful protest by Greenpeace led to its replacement with Teflon-coated fibreglass, adding £8 million to the cost.

The Dome was completed in time for a spectacular party celebrating the arrival of the new millennium, and is seen here during lighting rehearsals in December 1999 with the Thames Barrier lit up in the background. The Dome's changing colours were designed by Patrick Woodroffe, who cut his teeth lighting concerts for bands such as the Rolling Stones and Tina Turner, and could be seen as a metaphor for the chameleon-like way in which the political parties praised or poured scorn on the Dome depending on who was in power.

above
The Millennium Dome
under construction.
30th October 1997.

opposite
In the pink or feeling
blue? The Millennium
Dome showing off its
colours in rehearsals
during the run-up to the
millennium eve party.
The Dome was a
different colour each day
of the week during the
year 2000: blue on
Monday, magenta on
Tuesday, indigo on
Wednesday, green on
Thursday, yellow on
Friday, pink on Saturday
and purple on Sunday.
17th December 1999.

The night-time views of the Dome on the previous page were taken from Canada Tower, another of London's newest landmarks and forever destined to be misnamed Canary Wharf. Cesar Pelli's spectacular stainless steel and glass skyscraper towers 800 feet above the Isle of Dogs – it can be seen from as far afield as Kent and Essex, and since this photograph was taken it has been joined by another two thrusting monuments to commerce. The tower was financed by Olympia and York, a Canadian company, hence its official name, and it stands on Canary Wharf, hence its unofficial one – the wharf takes its name from the fact that tomatoes and bananas were once landed here from the Canary Islands.

Canada Tower is London's and Britain's tallest building, 200 feet taller than its predecessor for the title, Tower 42, seen here rising surreally above the more traditional City buildings as though it has been added to the set of a science fiction film by an over-enthusiastic designer. Tower 42 is yet another London landmark with an identity crisis, being almost universally known by its former title, the NatWest Tower. From the air, though not from this angle, it is clear that in plan the shape of the tower matches the logo of the National Westminster Bank. It stands on the site of Thomas Gresham's house, financial adviser to Elizabeth I and founder of the Royal Exchange, and was designed by R Seifert & Partners – when it was completed in 1980 it was the tallest building in Europe at 52 storeys, or 600 feet, high.

Just as Canada Tower superseded Tower 42 as London's tallest building, so Tower 42 superseded the BT Tower (still known to many people as the Post Office Tower), although the BT Tower still has a partial claim to outrank Tower 42 – the tower itself is 580 feet high but the weather radar aerial mounted on the roof is 40 feet high, giving an overall height of 620 feet.

The BT Tower is effectively a huge pylon built to support radio, television and telecoms aerials, and was designed by a team of architects from the Ministry of Works led by Eric Bedford. It was completed in 1965 and bombed anonymously in 1971; sadly, as a result, the tower and the revolving restaurant have been closed to the public since 1980.

left
Some things never
change... traffic chaos at
the Elephant and Castle.
June 1930.

below
The Elephant and Castle.
16th May 2000.

'Despite its comical name, Elephant and Castle is not much fun at all.' 20th–century commentator Rob Humphreys pulls no punches in his damnation of the Elephant and Castle, and 100 years earlier Dickens the younger was not much kinder, dismissing the Elephant and Castle Theatre as 'a transpontine house of no particular characteristic'.

Better known as a notoriously busy traffic junction than for any elephants or castles, the area takes its name from an 18th-century tavern which in turn is thought either to have been named after the sign of the Cutler's Company, which dealt in ivory, or to be a corruption of the Infanta of Castille, who was engaged to Charles I. The seemingly unorthodox arrangement of a castle on the back of an elephant was quite common in medieval heraldry, and in some chess sets the castle is carved on the back of an elephant. The tavern was used by archers from nearby Newington Butts (a butt is a raised mound used for archery practice); it became well known as a coaching inn during the 18th and 19th centuries and later became a terminus for trams.

The area around the Elephant and Castle was badly bombed during the Second World War, and was redeveloped from 1961–66 around a pair of enormous and confusing roundabouts. Chaotic and congested traffic is nothing new, however: an 1826 aquatint by Pollard shows a mêlée of dogs, horses and carriages thronging the area in front of the tavern much as the buses, vans and bicycles are doing in the 1930 photograph. A close look at the pre-war picture shows that there were even one or two horse-drawn carts still on the road.

There is a characterless modern pub called the *Elephant and Castle* at the top of the New Kent Road but today the area is dominated by an enormous pink shopping arcade designed by Boissevian and Osmond as part of the 1960s' redevelopment, its colour being the only thing preventing it from being very aptly described as a white elephant.

above

Battersea Power Station, still looking majestic despite being isolated in an industrial wasteland and partially dismantled. 12th January 1990.

opposite

Ingrid Sellscop, Robert Hyman, Susan Vale and Catherine Millligan play Haydn, not as an elegy to Battersea Power Station but to celebrate the re-opening of the site for redevelopment. 8th June 1988.

From pink elephants to Pink Floyd – in 1977 Battersea power station, seen above and right, featured on the cover of Pink Floyd's album *Animals* with a giant helium-filled pig attached to one of the chimneys. Designer Storm Thorgerson, co-founder of the design agency Hipgnosis, had not sought permission for this stunt and the first the authorities knew of it was when the pilot of a jumbo jet making his approach to Heathrow reported it to air traffic control (or so the story goes). Worse was to come because the giant pig then broke free from the chimney of the power station and was later recovered from a garden in Kent.

Battersea power station has been described as looking from a distance like an upturned snooker table and was designed by Sir Giles Gilbert Scott, whose other creations include Liverpool Cathedral and Waterloo Bridge. 'Station A' was opened in 1933 with one chimney at each end, and the power station was later doubled in size by the addition of 'Station B' which, although it began generating power in 1948, was not completed until 1953. The smoke that once issued from the four chimneys was a pristine white, having been 'washed' by special smoke-cleaning apparatus.

In 1983, just 30 years after it was completed, the entire edifice was shut down and partially dismantled. Five years later, on 8th June 1988, Prime Minister Margaret Thatcher, supported by lasers, pyrotechnics and a string quartet, officially re-opened the site for development as a leisure park, and three years after that it was once again abandoned when the developer ran out of money.

above

Bisected by the horizon
in this view from New
Zealand House, the
London Eye
revolutionises an idea
pioneered in Chicago in
1893 by George Ferris to
celebrate the 400th
anniversary of the arrival
of Columbus in the New
World.
9th December 1999.

Battersea Power Station was built to last but outlived its usefulness. It seems that the opposite may be true of the London Eye, which only has planning permission for five years. All the signs are that it will remain popular for much longer than that should it be allowed to stay, and it is already being talked of as London's Eiffel Tower which, similarly, was due to remain in place for only a few years after the Paris Exposition of 1889.

The Eye is the world's largest observation wheel, and was designed by husband-and-wife team Julia Barfield and David Marks as an entry for a competition organised in 1993 by *The Sunday Times* and the Architecture Foundation. The competition was held to find ideas for a monument to mark the new millennium but the judging panel was not as far-sighted as the organisers: the prize was not awarded because the judges decided that none of the entries was good enough! Thankfully Barfield and Marks did not give up, managed to secure commercial sponsorship, and provided London with its most elegant and exciting millennium landmark.

Julia Barfield says that the idea came about because they were looking for a structure that was massive but not dominating: 'We wanted it to be a light, airy structure, a sculpture on the skyline, and we wanted it to be white.' Another requirement was that the structure should provide a high viewpoint for a panorama of the city and, in David Marks' words, 'a wheel is not only a very efficient machine for getting people up to a high viewing platform but it could also turn continuously, so in addition it would be a symbol of time turning.'

Most London landmarks have had their supporters and their detractors but the London Eye, despite the initial reluctance of the prize committee and a few teething problems, seems to be almost universally popular. Not so the London Ark, which follows the more usual pattern of provoking a mixture of praise and complaints. Designed by Ralph Erskine and built from 1990–91, the interior of the Ark is flooded with natural light, and the windows are triple-glazed to keep energy in and noise out. The building is hailed in most quarters as a graceful and striking piece of architecture floating beside the ugly Hammersmith Flyover but local residents complain that while the interior may be noise-proof, the rattle and clatter of the trains snaking their way around the building en route to and from Hammersmith Broadway reverberates off the curved walls.

above
The ecologically designed London Ark, in Hammersmith. January 1992.

above
Members of the
Women's Institute
picnicking outside the
Albert Hall.
2nd July 1986.

opposite
HM The Queen and
Sir Jocelyn Stevens,
Chairman of English
Heritage, in the spotlight
at the unveiling of the
newly renovated Albert
Memorial.
21st October 1998.

Julia Barfield and David Marks turned to British Airways to finance the London Eye but over a century earlier, in the absence of such a corporate sponsor, the committee responsible for the Albert Hall had come up with a more ingenious way of raising money – a 999-year leasehold of seats. Over thirteen hundred seats were leased at a price of £100 each, which entitled the leaseholder to free attendance at every performance, and the scheme still holds good today. Queen Victoria bought 20 seats, which make up the current Royal Box, and the Commissioners of the Great Exhibition donated the site at a peppercorn rent of one shilling (10p) a year, still paid annually on 25th March.

As their names suggest, the Royal Albert Hall and the Albert Memorial, that stands across the road from it, were built in memory of Queen Victoria's beloved consort, Prince Albert. He had presided over a Royal Commission to set up the Great Exhibition of 1851, which was such a success that he was given the title Consort for his involvement with it. He used the profits to fulfil his dream of an establishment that would extend the influence of science and art to industry, and set about creating 'Albertropolis', the area of South Kensington that is now home to the Victoria & Albert Museum, the Science Museum and the Natural History Museum.

After Albert's death a public fund was set up to finance a memorial and to realise his dream of a hall with libraries, exhibition rooms and an enormous lecture theatre, though what he would have thought of its use a century later for concerts by Bob Dylan, Eric Clapton and Deep Purple, or as a big top for Cirque du Soleil, can only be imagined.

The Albert Memorial was designed by George Gilbert Scott, grandfather of Giles Gilbert Scott, the architect of Battersea Power Station. Queen Victoria never expressed an opinion of the monument but her feelings were made clear when Scott was knighted soon after its completion. The monument had no official unveiling ceremony but that omission was compensated for in fine style more than a century later when, on 21st October 1998, HM The Queen unveiled the restored Albert Memorial following four years of renovation by English Heritage.

The hall itself was designed by another Scott, Colonel H.Y. Darracott Scott, and when the foundation stone was laid by Queen Victoria she surprised everyone by adding the words 'Royal Albert' to the hall's intended title, which was to have been the Central Hall of Arts and Sciences. At the opening ceremony four years later she was so overcome with emotion that the Prince of Wales had to step forward and declare the hall officially open on behalf of his mother. It is said that Victoria's grief at the loss of her beloved husband is the origin of the 'royal we', because after Albert's death the Queen continued to refer to herself as if he was still beside her.

London

Icons

02

THE WORD 'ICON' COMES FROM the Greek *eikon*, meaning an image or likeness. Originally used to describe religious icons, usually of Christ or the saints, the meaning of the word has broadened to mean not just a likeness of something but an image or object that is representative of something. It is in this broader sense that the following 'London icons' have been chosen, not just because they are unique to the capital but also because they are symbols of the traditions, history and people that make London what it is.

Just as with religious icons, cheap copies of many of these London icons can be seen every day in gift shops and tourist-traps: plastic trinkets representing the things that instantly say 'London' to a visitor – Big Ben in a snow shaker, a black cab fridge magnet, a plastic policeman's helmet, a toy London bus. Many of the things that could be considered iconic of London are also landmarks (St Paul's, Tower Bridge, Nelson's Column) but London is not just bricks and mortar, there are also groups of people whose presence tells visitors that they are in London as surely as any street sign – Beefeaters, Chelsea Pensioners, the Pearly Kings and Queens.

There is one famous London family whose home at the end of the Mall is recognised across the world but it is often forgotten that London also has another, working class, royalty: the Pearly Kings and Queens. Instantly recognisable by the countless pearl buttons sewn onto their clothes, this alternative royalty has its roots in a far less sparkling trade: the costermongers of the Middle Ages. Costermongering (selling wares, usually food, from a barrow in the streets) was an exhausting, highly competitive and sometimes dangerous trade that involved pushing a heavy barrow through the poorest parts of London, sometimes covering 10 miles in a 12- to 14-hour day.

As well as the dangers of the streets, costermongers had to cope with an influx of unemployed workers 'taking to the barrow' and with the inevitable bullies and cheats who would take the best pitches and exploit the weak. Costermongering was unlicensed, which meant that although the authorities turned a blind eye to the practice (they realised the necessity of the trade both for those employed and those served by it), costermongers could not expect any legal protection. For this reason the costermongers of each borough elected a leader to protect their rights and settle disputes; each leader became the local 'king' and this 'regional royalty' evolved into the Pearly Kings and Queens. The tradition continues today, although they now devote their time to charitable work rather than the rougher side of street trading.

right
Len Pearsen, James
Griffen, Arthur Jeffrey,
Ron Smith and Eddy Lee
taking advantage of an
offer by Merrill Lynch
allowing needy senior
citizens to make free
phone calls to anywhere
in the world.
13th December 1998.

Although the coster royalty had been evolving since the Middle Ages, the Pearly Kings' and Queens' Association was not formed until 1911. More than two hundred years earlier another institution was founded whose members were to become a familiar and much-loved sight on the streets of the capital – the Chelsea Hospital.

The Royal Hospital (to give it its official title) was founded in 1682 by Charles II as a retirement home for veteran soldiers. Legend has it that he was persuaded to do so by Nell Gwynn, who had been distressed by the sight of an old soldier begging on the King's Road. It is true that she was one of the original patrons, donating £200 to the cause, but it is more likely that the King was following the example of Louis XIV's Hôtel des Invalides in Paris. The Hospital was designed by Sir Christopher Wren and the first Pensioners took up residence in 1689, three years before it was actually completed.

There are about 420 'in-pensioners' who live on the premises, all men over 65 (or over 55 if they are unable to earn a living) who have been injured on active service. Pensioners are given board, lodging, clothing, a small weekly allowance and nursing care if they are ill. They must wear a blue uniform

with a peaked cap at all times within a one-mile radius of the Hospital, and wear the familiar scarlet uniform further afield and on special occasions. A three-cornered hat is worn on ceremonial occasions such as Founder's Day, known as Oak Apple Day, which is held annually on the anniversary of Charles II's birth on 29th May 1630. On Oak Apple Day the Pensioners also wear an oak leaf in remembrance of the fact that the King escaped with his life by hiding in the Boscobel Oak after defeat at the Battle of Worcester in 1651.

There have been three women Pensioners in the history of the Hospital, one of whom, Hannah Snell, joined the army as James Gray; she had no difficulty with the enrolment, which consisted of kissing the flag, taking the King's shilling and drinking a pint of beer – there was no medical. When she was eventually discovered as a woman she deserted and joined the Royal Marines during which time she was wounded, qualifying her to be a Chelsea Pensioner. Under the Duke of Cumberland's influence she was awarded 'out-pensioner' status and wore her blue uniform while running her pub in Wapping, called *The Female Warrior*.

above

Chelsea Pensioners George Hatton, 97, formerly of the Royal Fusiliers, and Dick Collins, 95, formerly of the East Lancashire Regimement, on Oak Apple Day at the Royal Hospital, Chelsea. 7th June 1990.

A female warrior of a different kind to Hannah Snell (previous page) was the last person to be locked up in a small cell within St Stephen's Tower, the Clock Tower of the Houses of Parliament, better known as Big Ben. The cell was built to imprison unruly members of Parliament or agitators causing trouble within the Palace of Westminster. The last time an MP was locked up there was in 1880, but in 1902 it was used to confine Emmeline Pankhurst, the leader of the suffragette movement.

Mike McCann, the current Keeper of the Great Clock, says 'I once read that Big Ben is the most widely recognised building on the planet' and yet, like so many of London's towers, it is known by the incorrect name. 'Big Ben' originally referred not to the clock or the tower but to the 13.5-ton bell, whose chime is familiar across the globe to listeners of the BBC World Service – every hourly chime heard on the World Service since 1934 has been broadcast live from a microphone in the tower. There are two theories as to the origin of the name, one being that it was named after Sir Benjamin Hall, Chief Commissioner of Works at the time it was made, the other that it was named after Benjamin Caunt, a popular heavyweight boxer who weighed over two hundred and fifty pounds.

The tower was designed by Sir Charles Barry, who won a competition to design new buildings for the Houses of Parliament after the greater part of the Palace of Westminster burned to the ground in 1834. Barry wanted the Queen's clockmaker to design the clock, which was to be 'a noble clock... indeed a king of clocks, the biggest and best in the world, within sight and sound of the throbbing heart of London'. However, after much argument, the clock was made by E.J. Dent to the designs of Edmund Beckett Denison, a lawyer, MP, and amateur watchmaker.

Denison's clock met very stringent conditions for accuracy and nearly a century and a half later, on the eve of the new millennium, chimed within one-tenth of a second of the Atomic Clock. But while his design for the clock was a great success the same could not be said of his efforts with the bell.

Against the advice of the bellfounders, Denison insisted on the wrong mixture of metals, and then increased the size of the hammer from 7cwt to 13cwt, causing a four-foot crack in the already weak bell, which had to be recast. The new bell was hauled by 16 white horses from the Whitechapel Bell Foundry and installed in the clock tower but within a few months Big Ben developed a large crack. To crack one bell may be regarded as a misfortune, to crack two looks like carelessness, and indeed it was: investigation showed that Denison had repeated his mistake, having increased the size of the hammer to 7cwt from the 4cwt stipulated, and Big Ben has chimed slightly out of tune ever since.

above
A sightseeing boat
passing the Palace of
Westminster.
11th April 1999.

right
Traditional Routemaster
buses on Oxford Street.
18th March 1996.

One person rarely out of tune is Sir Andrew Lloyd-Webber, whose musicals have redefined West End Theatre – and the livery of London's buses. The traditional Routemaster bus, seen here, is so closely identified with the capital that it is known to most people simply as 'the London bus'.

The word 'omnibus' was introduced to Britain by George Shillibeer, who set up London's first bus service in 1829 between Paddington and Bank. Until then those who were rich enough used their own carriages, or hired hackneys or hansom cabs, and everyone else had to walk. Shillibeer's service justified the name 'omnibus' (meaning 'for all' in Latin) because in theory passengers could join the vehicle along the route, but horse-drawn buses remained a particularly middle-class form of transport because most services started at 8 a.m., long after the working classes were at work.

Buses quickly became so popular, and so crowded, that passengers took to sitting on the roof, which was such common practice by the 1850s that seats were provided for them and the double-decker was born. And with these lofty seats came 'decency boards', placed along the side of the roof to prevent young men from glimpsing the ankles of any ladies riding on the top deck. Advertisers soon took advantage of decency boards as mobile hoardings, providing the forerunner of the Lloyd Webber advertisements seen here.

Horse-drawn buses eventually gave way to the internal combustion engine, and London Transport began to design buses specifically to meet its needs. The Routemaster is the culmination of this process, the last bus to be designed 'in-house' by LT and the last of the traditional open rear platform buses to remain in service in Britain. The separate driver's cab is a reminder of the days when the driver had an exterior perch from which to control the horses. The Routemaster is still seen by many as the ideal bus for London, with the open rear platform allowing fast loading and unloading, and giving passengers the chance to hop on and off in the slow-moving traffic. Its very popularity with the public has slowed down its planned replacement by modern 'single-manned' buses.

Although the omnibus brought transport to the masses its arrival did not kill off the cab trade, and the London taxi is still as much a part of the city streets as it ever was. While other cities use production cars with meters attached London is the only city in the world to have its own purpose-designed taxicab, which is why the black cab (and even its multi-coloured variants) has become such an evocative icon of the city.

Like the Routemaster, the old-style taxis are so popular that they are only slowly being replaced. The Austin FX4 has graced the streets of the capital since 1958, and is now being replaced by the ugly, box-like Metrocab and the more traditional lines of the TX1; if the TX1 lasts as long as the FX4, it will still be sharing the streets with its successor in 2044.

below left
Carnaby Street, whose
street sign was once
London's most popular
postcard.
1st September 1996.

below
Dedicated Followers of
Fashion – ra-ra skirts
and bobble hats on the
street that paved the
way for fashion for more
than a decade.
25th November 1987.

In the spring of 1966 *The Times* ran a front-page headline that read: 'London – The Swinging City'. In the article that accompanied it *The Times*' London correspondent claimed that 'in this century every decade has had its city… today it is London, a city steeped in tradition, seized by change, liberated by affluence… In a decade dominated by youth, London has burst into bloom. It swings, it is the scene.'

During the 'Swinging Sixties' Carnaby Street, along with the King's Road, was synonymous with this 'London scene'. The myth had begun a few years earlier in 1957 when John Stephen, John Vince and Andreas Spyropoulos started selling flamboyant men's clothes to the Soho gay community. Their shop *Vince* was so successful that it was quickly followed by others, and Carnaby Street was soon transformed from a row of tailoring sweatshops into a parade of trendy boutiques.

Carnaby Street made its mark just as the 1960s started swinging, and by 1964 it was the place to be seen: it had entered the *Oxford English Dictionary* as a noun meaning 'fashionable clothing for young people'; the *Daily Telegraph* pointed out for those who might not have noticed that it was the place where 'switched-on people' would hang out, and the street sign became London's most popular postcard, almost the definition of a London Icon. But the magic didn't last and Carnaby Street failed to move with the times, unlike the King's Road, which embraced the 'Chelsea Set' of the 1960s, became the birthplace of punk in the 1970s, and where 'Laura Ashley' now sells fabrics in premises formerly used by Thomas Crapper to produce toilets. Having set the trends for a decade or more, Carnaby Street was left behind by them and, despite Sixties' fashion guru Mary Quant opening a shop there in 1987, has now become almost as reliable a word for tackiness as it once was for trendiness.

For those who prefer their shopping traditional rather than trendy, London has a host of department stores whose names are as much a part of the city's story as the names of its architects and institutions. The most recent of the big three seen here is the creation of an American who came to London from Chicago to make his fortune and, yes, they do sell fridges.

Harry Gordon Selfridge's dream was to create a department store that stretched from Oxford Street to Wigmore Street with a dome as big as St Paul's, and he achieved it, except for the dome. The store opened for business on 15th March 1909 and the first item sold was a handkerchief, for 1s4d, to a Madam Barry of Bond Street. In the course of building his empire the Chief, as Selfridge was known, pioneered many retailing firsts including the bargain basement, in-store credit, putting the perfume counter near the entrance to entice customers in from the street, and the coining of the all-too familiar phrase 'only 10 more shopping days to Christmas'.

Sixty years older than Selfridges is Harrods, which came into being in 1849 when Charles Henry Harrod, a wholesale tea merchant, took over a small grocer's shop in Knightsbridge. His son Charles Digby Harrod bought the shop from his father and built up the business, attracting account customers who included Oscar Wilde, Lillie Langtry and Ellen Terry. Before Selfridges had even opened, Harrods had claimed its own significant 'first', opening London's first escalator in 1898; attendants were stationed at the top to hand out smelling salts and brandy to nervous customers. The famous terracotta façade was begun three years later in 1901 and, a century later, is lit every night by 11,500 light bulbs. Harrods was bought by House of Fraser in 1959 but became a family firm again in 1985 when it was bought for £615 million by the Fayed brothers. Mohamed Al Fayed tells prospective customers in the foreword to the store's guide book: 'Rest assured you will always be made welcome at the Palace in Knightsbridge.'

Fortnum & Mason's pedigree goes back more than a hundred years earlier still, and leaves even Harrods looking a little down-market. It was established in the 1770s by Charles Fortnum, who was a footman to George III. One of Fortnum's duties was to replenish the royal candelabra, and his retail experience began with selling the used candles to the Queen's Ladies-in-Waiting. After leaving the royal household he set up in business with his partner Hugh Mason and the shop became an instant success, importing exotic foods through the East India Company, supplying gentlemen's clubs such as the Athenaeum and Boodle's, and, in 1886, having the foresight to buy up the entire stock of newly invented canned food produced by a certain Mr Heinz.

Just along Piccadilly from Fortnum & Mason's is the Ritz Hotel, which is named after Swiss hotelier César Ritz, one-time manager of the nearby Savoy Hotel, and which has been 'a byword for decadence since it first wowed Edwardian society in 1906'. The word ritzy is still a colloquialism for anything high-class, stylish or ostentatiously rich (or all three), and tea at the Ritz, seen by many as the ultimate extravagance, is so oversubscribed that those not on the A-list must book several weeks in advance.

The hotel was designed by architects Mewès and Davis, who designed the Paris Ritz, and the arcade of the Piccadilly façade is based on the buildings of the Rue de Rivoli. Tea is served in the opulent Palm Court, while for those with enough money left after the sandwiches, scones, clotted cream, jam, and cakes, the best rooms are to the west, overlooking Green Park. The interior of the hotel is in the style of Louis XVI, with bespoke furniture made by Waring and Gillow to the designs of the architects.

Robert Gillow established a workshop on Oxford Street in the 1760s on the site of what is now Selfridges, making furniture with his brothers. S.J. Waring was a Liverpool cabinet maker who set up near Marble Arch in 1895 and merged with Gillow's in 1906, the year that the Ritz opened. Together the partnership made furniture for gentlemen's clubs such as Boodle's, the Garrick and the Reform, as well as for the private apartments at Windsor Castle and for London's top hotels, including the Carlton and the Ritz.

Just like the city's institutions and department stores, London's hotels have their part to add to the story of the capital: tea at the Ritz is an institution in itself; the Langham Hotel appears in several Sherlock Holmes stories and played host to Toscanini, Dvořák, Napoleon III and Haile Selassie; the Carlton was opened by César Ritz, who had a nervous breakdown when his planned 1902 season was ruined by the postponement of Edward VII's coronation; staff at the Hyde Park Hotel milked a goat each day for Mahatma Gandhi when he stayed there, and the Savoy, built on the site of a medieval palace, employed Guccio Gucci as a dishwasher, provided Monet with a window from which to paint the Thames and, perhaps most significantly of all, created a new dessert, the peach Melba, for Dame Nellie Melba when she was a guest there.

above

The Ritz Hotel, built to the specifications of César Ritz by the designers of the Paris Ritz, its arcade echoing the Rue de Rivoli.
12th July 1990.

opposite

A tea dance at the Ritz. Tea in the mirrored Palm Court at the Ritz is an extravagance reminiscent of the mythical 'Edwardian summer' during which the hotel was built.
30th May 1985.

London's

03

River

below

A carthorse cooling off in the Thames, with the Palace of Westminster in view beyond Lambeth Bridge. 31st May 1937.

'THAMES' IS THE OLDEST DOCUMENTED place name in British history after Kent, having been first recorded in the account of Julius Caesar's invasion c55BC as *Tamesis*. Little is known of the history of London before that point but what is known is that the river was of vital importance for both the Celts and the Romans in the development of the town that became London. The Celts settled around the natural harbour of the Pool of London while the Romans, when they returned in force under the Emperor Claudius eight years later in 43BC, built a bridge there. It was this first bridge that led to the rapid development of London, and within a decade it was a thriving settlement.

The Thames was London's lifeblood, providing water for drinking and washing, fish for food, power for mills and a tidal port for international trade and commerce. The river also provided a means of transport and travel at a time when more people owned a boat than a horse and cart, although several

centuries later the carter in this photograph seems to want the best of both worlds. (In fact he is probably about to unload a barge which, even as late as the 1930s, were beached on the river bank and unloaded into carts at low tide.)

In 1632 Donald Lupton called the Thames 'a broad slippery fellow', and wrote that 'merchandise he likes and loves; and therefore sends ships to most parts of the earth… the city is wondrously beholden to it, for she is furnished with almost all necessaries by it'. And thanks to the broad slippery fellow London continued to grow: by 1700 the city's docks were handling fully 80 per cent of the country's imports and 69 per cent of its exports, with goods arriving from the East and West Indies, Africa, North America and the Baltic, making London truly 'the heart of empire'.

The first of London's enclosed wet docks, the Howland, was built in 1697 in Rotherhithe to accommodate some of this trade and Rotherhithe Street, to the north of the Howland, found itself with water on both sides as the docks expanded to become the Surrey Commercial Docks. The 18th-century houses in the photograph of Rotherhithe Street above were about to be demolished but *The Angel* tavern adjoining them survived the demolition; it dates back to the 15th century when the monks of Bermondsey Abbey kept a tavern there and, like the houses in the picture, is partly built on piles over the river. *The Angel* did its bit for London's unofficial traders, who were also thriving, with smuggler's trapdoors opening over the water below.

above
These houses adjoining *The Angel* tavern in Rotherhithe were about to be demolished, and were the last remaining 18th-century houses abutting the southern foreshore of the Pool of London. January 1938.

As well as providing a livelihood for those living alongside it, the Thames is literally home to a select band of people who live on its waters. The three-bedroom house sailing through Tower Bridge, fully furnished and complete with garage and front- and back-gardens, is on its way to an exhibition at Thames moorings but the houseboats seen here at the Beaufort Stairs Wharf in Chelsea are genuine homes – the price of one of these houseboats includes a licence to moor it here at one of 58 permanent moorings owned and served by the Chelsea Yacht and Boat Company. The moorings are divided between the Beaufort Stairs Wharf in the foreground and the Chelsea Wharf beyond, both of them beside Cheyne Walk in Chelsea but, confusingly, on the Battersea Reach of the Thames (the Chelsea Reach ends at Battersea Bridge).

The Chelsea Yacht and Boat Company was established in 1935 on the site of an earlier boatyard founded here in the 19th century, and was reorganised during the 1980s and '90s with new moorings, improved mains water and power supplies, and pontoon access to all the houseboats. Today 'Chelsea Yacht' is a family-run company employing about a dozen people, but during the Second World War the workforce swelled to over one hundred as the company carried out contracts for the Admiralty. Chelsea Yacht supplied small boats for the evacuation of Dunkirk in 1940, and later in the war Admiralty work included converting Thames lighters and dumb barges for use in Operation Overlord: landing craft and support craft sailed from the moorings seen here to play a vital part in the success of the landings on Sword Beach in Normandy.

After the war a number of landing craft and motor torpedo boats (including MTB 219 which took

right
Tower Bridge has opened many times in its 100-plus years, but rarely to let a fully furnished, brick-built, three-bedroom house sail through.
9th September 1974.

part in the attack on the *Scharnhorst*) returned to Chelsea where they were converted into houseboats. Many of them have since been replaced by converted Thames lighters and Dutch barges but a close inspection shows that some of the assault landing craft were 'slipped' into steel hulls specially designed and built by Chelsea Yacht to prolong their life, and they are still in use today, having been refitted as special 46-foot houseboats.

During the 1950s the company entered the world of show business, building a fully operational Missouri paddle steamer called *Showboat* for the Festival of Britain celebrations at the Battersea Pleasure Gardens, and providing a film location for *Naked Truth*, which saw Peter Sellers and Terry Thomas clowning around on the pontoons and houseboats.

left
Homes with a difference – these houseboats at the Beaufort Stairs Wharf in Chelsea are alternately rocked by the tide and gently beached on the foreshore every few hours.
8th June 1999.

below
The Chief Warder of the
Tower of London builds
sandcastles with
children who went to
play on Tower Beach on
the day it reopened after
the war. 9th July 1945.

opposite
'London by the Sea' –
Londoners make the
most of the sunshine on
Tower Beach, close to
the Tower of London and
Tower Bridge.
18th May 1952.

As recently as the 1950s the beaches on the Thames foreshore were a popular place for 'stay-at-home Londoners' to relax, although the river is now so polluted that few people would think of lying on the sand to sunbathe, much less swimming in the river.

The practice of relaxing on the Thames beaches goes back at least as far as the 11th century, when King Canute famously tried to stop the tide on the foreshore at Westminster. According to the 16th century historian John Norden, Canute 'passed by the Thamys, which ran by that Pallace, at the flowing of the tide; and making staie neere the water, the waves cast some part of their water towards him. This Canutus conjured the waves by his regal commande to proceed no farther. The Thamas, unacquainted with this new god, held on its course, flowing as of custome it used to do and refrained not to assayle him neere to the knees'.

The popular interpretation of this tale is that Canute thought he had the powers of a god and was surprised when the waves did not obey him, but that would be out of character for a man who 'showed reverence and generosity to the Church and its native saints'. (Canute, or Knut Sveinsson, was not a native; he was Danish, and was king of Denmark and Norway as well as England.) The other version of the story is that Canute was fed up with his courtiers' belief that the King had divine powers and was trying to demonstrate that the waves would not obey his command. But actions speak louder than words, and Canute will always be remembered as the king who thought that he could control the tide.

There may be a return to beaches in the city, possibly initiated by politicians who would like to make waves, if not control the tide of public opinion. In the debate surrounding what to do with the Millennium Dome a suggestion published in one newspaper was to turn it into a massive indoor beach to rival the Ocean Dome in Miyazaki, Japan, complete with artificial sand, chlorinated water, a retractable roof for the odd occasion when the sun shines – and, of course, a wave machine.

below
London and Southwark
Bridges are clogged with
traffic heading into the
City, while trains roll
across the railway bridge
into Cannon Street
Station. 21st June 1989.

But it was bridges, not beaches, that made the Thames a workable river for a capital city. Bridges have always been vital for access and communications across the river, and it was the Roman bridge at the Pool of London that sparked off the initial growth of the city. It is remarkable that London Bridge (the original wooden bridge and its successors) remained the only bridge across the Thames downstream of Kingston until 1750, when Westminster Bridge was completed.

Looking at the commuters and cars streaming across London Bridge towards the City in these photographs, it is hard to imagine the bridge's 11th-century wooden predecessor being scuppered by King Aethelred and his ally King Olaf of Norway in order to defeat the Danish Vikings who had captured it; Olaf's destruction of the bridge is the origin of the nursery rhyme 'London Bridge is Falling Down'. The first stone bridge, begun in 1176, was considered 'one of the marvels of Christendom' and was built on 19 stone arches, one of which had a drawbridge to let large ships pass through. It was a 'living bridge' with shops and tall houses at each side of the roadway and fortified gates at each end, where the tarred heads of traitors were displayed on spikes as a deterrent to others.

Nearly six hundred years later the decaying buildings were removed from the old London Bridge when it was repaired in 1757–59, and in 1823–31 a new bridge was built by Sir John Rennie to his late father's design. Rennie's bridge was bought for $2.4 million by an American businessman and now spans a lake in Lake Havasu City, Arizona.

The present London Bridge was built from 1967–72 by Mott, Hay & Anderson and is seen here choked with traffic in the morning rush hour – those who tried driving across Southwark Bridge, in the background, fared little better on their journey to work. The recent history of Southwark Bridge, like its traffic, is similar to that of London Bridge: the original was built by John Rennie Snr from 1814–19 and it was rebuilt by Mott & Hay in 1912–21. Between the two road bridges is the railway bridge serving Cannon Street Station, built at the same time as the station and opened in 1866. New bridges and railways built during the 19th century did not just mean better communications for London, they also meant the further expansion of the capital; the bridges led to urban expansion southwards, while the arrival of the railways led to the new phenomenon of commuter suburbs.

above

The original Waterloo Bridge was closed to traffic in 1934 so that workmen could begin demolishing it. The temporary bridge alongside remained open to one-way traffic. 22nd June 1934.

The building of Vauxhall, Waterloo and Southwark Bridges in 1816, 1817 and 1819 respectively led to a sudden acceleration in the growth of south London, and turned Camberwell from 'a pleasant retreat of those citizens who have a taste for the country whilst their avocations daily call them to town' into another part of the town from which it had hitherto been a retreat.

Waterloo Bridge, like London and Southwark Bridges, was designed by John Rennie, and it was a great source of wonder and patriotic pride when it was opened by the Prince Regent on 18th June 1817, the second anniversary of the Battle of Waterloo. The Italian sculptor Canova called it 'the noblest bridge in the world, worth a visit from the remotest corner of the earth', while the government changed its name from the intended Strand Bridge in an 1816 Act of Parliament because 'the said bridge when completed will be a work of great stability and magnificence, and such works are adapted to transmit to posterity the remembrance of great and glorious achievements'.

However, stability and magnificence did not last as long as the remembrance of Waterloo because in 1923 two of the piers subsided and a temporary bridge had to be built alongside, seen here in 1934. Rennie's bridge, 'the handsomest across the Thames', was demolished amid great protest and rebuilt

in 1937–42 to the design of Sir Giles Gilbert Scott, famous for such London landmarks as Battersea Power Station, Bankside Power Station (now the Tate Modern) and the rather smaller K6, better known as the traditional red telephone box. (The K6 was a 'new look' designed in 1935 especially to celebrate the Silver Jubilee of George V, and 2,400 of them are now listed buildings.)

One of London's prettiest and most unusual bridges, beautifully lit at night, is Albert Bridge on the Chelsea Reach of the Thames, built by Roland Mason Ordish in 1871–73 under the principles of his 'straight-link suspension' system. This was a strange hybrid of cantilever and suspension, supported by wrought-iron bars radiating from the ornamental cast-iron towers, with vertical steel suspenders hung from the wrought-iron bars. The system was not wholly successful and Albert Bridge was overhauled in 1884 by Sir Joseph Bazalgette, Chief Engineer of the Metropolitan Board of Works, who strengthened it by the more conventional means of adding suspension cables. (Bazalgette designed or altered a total of five Thames bridges.) Ordish's wrought-iron bars and Bazalgette's suspension cables are now adorned with hundreds of light bulbs, emphasizing the unusual design of the bridge and making it even more striking at night than it is by day.

above
New lights decorate the suspension cables and ironwork of Albert Bridge. 26th November 1991.

below
Fireboat *The London Phoenix* passes under Tower Bridge on its way to launch a new mascot for the Fire Services Benevolent Fund. 18th May 1998.

The river in the 18th century was a chaotic place and rife with criminal activity. The docks could not cope with the huge amount of goods being imported and the line of ships waiting to be unloaded often stretched two miles above London Bridge and four miles below, with ships four or five deep at the moorings and more than three thousand wherries and lighters ferrying cargo and people to and from the busy wharves. In the midst of this chaos pirates would strip ships, anchors and all, 'scuffle hunters' would steal unguarded wares from the quayside and 'mud-larks' would collect goods from the water's edge that had been thrown overboard by accomplices.

Commercial losses became so great that the West India Company approached magistrate Dr Patrick Colquhon for advice on how to deal with the problem, and in 1798 Colquhon and John Harriot set up the River Police, the first fully organised police force in the country, predating the Metropolitan Police by 31 years. The River Police had stations at Wapping, Waterloo and Blackwall from which they

mounted six-hour patrols every two hours, day and night, in rowing galleys and sailing cutters – today they have a fleet of fast cruisers based mainly at Wapping. In 1839 the River Police were incorporated into the Met and became known as the Thames Division, and today any police officer wanting to transfer to Thames Division must serve two years on the beat and then complete a one-year intensive course before taking to the water.

Another emergency service with vessels on the Thames is the London Fire Brigade, which originated in the fire insurance companies that set up in the City after the Great Fire. The insurance companies realised that it was in their own interests to employ a team of men to put out fires in the buildings they insured, and issued every policyholder with a metal 'fire-marker' to fix to the outside of their property; fire brigades arriving at a property marked with the badge of a rival company would leave the fire to burn. Eventually the separate fire brigades began to co-operate and in 1833 they formed the London Fire Engine Establishment, which became the basis of the Metropolitan Fire Brigade, established in 1865 and renamed the London Fire Brigade in 1904. In 1887 the Brigade's water-borne equipment included four river fire stations, five steam fire engines on barges, five steam tugs, nine barges and sixteen pilots; today it has one river fire station, at Lambeth, and two fireboats, one of which is seen here at Tower Bridge in 1998.

above
Members of the River Police, officially known as the Thames Division, in one of their fast launches close to Tower Bridge. 1st January 2000.

opposite top
A.E. Gobbett from
Blackwall, winner of the
annual Doggett's Coat
and Badge Race, is
congratulated by a past
winner. 31st July 1935.

opposite bottom
The start of the
Doggett's Coat and
Badge Race at London
Bridge. The race has
been contested annually
since 1716.
30th July 1949.

right
The Oxford crew
approaching
Hammersmith Bridge:
R.A. Wheadon, bow,
E.V. Vine, J.A. Gobbo,
R.D.T. Raikes,
H.M.C. Quick,
J. McLeod, E.O.G. Pain,
J.J.H. Harrison, stroke,
W.R. Marsh, cox.
April 1954.

The first men to be recruited by the insurance companies as firefighters came from the ranks of the watermen, who for centuries had ferried people up, down and across the river. In general travel by water was the safest, cheapest and quickest means of transport but as the river became busier it also became more dangerous for passengers. Although most watermen were experienced, the crews of ships awaiting a berth in the port of London would often act as amateur watermen despite not knowing the local tides and not being used to handling small boats. Furthermore, Londoners would often bet on races between watermen, which meant that they built lighter and narrower boats which were less safe for passengers. All of this resulted in Henry VIII passing an Act establishing the Watermen's Company, which inspected and licensed the boats (to be a minimum size of 20ft 6ins long and 4ft 6ins wide), regulated apprenticeships, fixed fares and administered discipline.

One waterman's tradition that continues to this day is the Doggett's Coat and Badge Race, the oldest annually contested sporting event in the country. The race was first rowed in 1716 and was set up by Thomas Doggett, a comedian and joint manager of the Drury Lane Theatre, whose will provided for the prize of a coat and badge: 'ffive pounds for a badge of silver weighing about twelve ounces...

eighteen shillings for Cloath for a livery, whereon the said badge is to be put, one pound one shilling for making up the said Livery and Buttons… all of which I would have to be continued yearly in commemoration of His Majesty King George's happy accession to the British throne.'

It is said that the reason Doggett chose to commemorate George I's accession in this way was that late one night, drunk and in terrible weather, Doggett was having difficulty finding a waterman to row him home the four-and-a-half miles from London Bridge to Chelsea; eventually a new apprentice agreed to take him and in gratitude he set up the race, which is rowed over that course.

The more famous boat race is also rowed over a four-and-a-half mile course, from Putney to Mortlake; the 1954 Oxford crew is seen opposite approaching Hammersmith Bridge. The University Boat Race, so-named despite the fact that only two universities actually compete, has been rowed in London since 1845, becoming an annual event in 1856 and increasing in popularity towards the end of the century until it was said that 'every tint and shade and film of shade of Gainsborough's *Blue Boy* was patched upon the myriads who covered the Thames valley from Putney to Mortlake'.

opposite
The start of the
Mumm Champagne
London–Calais–London
offshore power boat
race. 13th July 1986.

above
Competitors in the City
of London's Festival
Regatta, having raced
from Putney Bridge,
await the signal for the
start of the return race
back to Putney.
21st July 1962.

As well as being the annual starting point for the University Boat Race, Putney Bridge also saw the start of the City of London's Festival Regatta in 1962, when more than three hundred yachts in seven classes raced from Putney Bridge to Tower Bridge – here they are seen gathering at Tower Bridge for a return race to Putney. Almost exactly three hundred years earlier the first documented yacht race in British waters took place on the Thames when in 1661 Charles II raced his brother James from Greenwich to Gravesend and back, winning both the race and a bet of £100.

The Thames had a continuing place in yachting history: the 'Cumberland Fleet' held some of the country's earliest regattas on the river above Blackfriars, and one of Britain's oldest existing yacht clubs is the Royal Thames Yacht Club, which was founded as a breakaway from the Cumberland Fleet after 'violent disagreements at the regatta held in 1823 to commemorate the coronation of George IV'. George IV was himself a keen yachtsman and, as Prince Regent, had joined the Yacht Club in Cowes on the Isle of Wight, which became the Royal Yacht Club and later, in 1833, the Royal Yacht Squadron.

Somewhat less sedate is the start of the London-Calais-London offshore power-boat race passing under Tower Bridge in 1986. Power was an anathema to traditional yachtsmen, and in 1827 the Royal Yacht Club passed a resolution that 'the object of this club is to promote seamanship to which the application of steam is inimical, and any member applying steam to his yacht shall be disqualified hereby and shall cease to be a member'. Steam yachts were said to be 'more popular with the ladies, who in general preferred the stately progression available with the steam engine to the hurly-burly of sail' (ask round-the-world yachtswoman Tracy Edwards!), but the advent of the internal combustion engine completely removed power-boat racing from the world of yachting.

In 1905 the first London-to-Cowes power boat race was held, which became an annual event until the outbreak of war in 1914. After the war the technology that had gone into designing motor torpedo boats was applied to racing boats, and courses became much longer: in 1972 a 14-stage London-to-Monaco power boat race was held, with 11 boats out of 20 completing the 2,700-mile course, making this return journey to Calais look like a mere shopping trip.

above

The 3,000-ton *Sand Kite*
lies half submerged after
hitting the Thames
Barrier in thick fog.
27th October 1997.

opposite

A competitor in the
Thames Oyster Smack
Race passes through the
flood barrier.
1st September 1989.

Competitors in the 1972 London-to-Monaco race would have been among the last to race down the Thames without the obstacle of the Thames Flood Barrier, the construction of which was begun three years later and completed in 1982; it was certainly a barrier to the skipper of the 3,000 tonne *Sand Kite*, which hit one of the machine housings in thick fog in 1997.

The Thames Barrier, described by the Queen at the opening ceremony in 1983 as 'the Eighth Wonder of the World', is not only a stunning piece of architecture but also a remarkable feat of engineering, most of which is hidden under water. The Barrier is 520 metres wide, and between the machine housings are 10 retractable steel gates which lie in concrete sills on the river bed and take about thirty minutes to raise. Each of the four main gates is as high as a five-storey building, as wide as the opening of Tower Bridge, and weighs over three thousand tons.

London has been subject to flooding throughout its history. The earliest record of a Thames flood is dated 1099, when 'on the festival of St Martin, the sea flood sprung up to such a height and did so much harm as no man remembered that it ever did before'; in 1236, 'in the great Palace of Westminster men did row with wherries in the midst of the Hall', and in 1633 Samuel Pepys wrote that 'there was last night the greatest tide that ever was remembered in England to have been in this river, all Whitehall being drowned'.

During the 20th century, until the building of the Thames Barrier, the danger of a catastrophic flood was more severe than at any time in history, for three reasons: sea levels are rising due to the melting of the polar ice caps, Britain is tilting towards the south-east at a rate of one foot every 100 years, and London is slowly sinking into its soft clay foundations. This combination of factors means that Thames tides are effectively rising by over two feet every century and only one thing stands between London and the might of nature – all hail Rendel, Palmer & Tritton, the engineers of the Thames Barrier, who seem to have achieved what Canute could not.

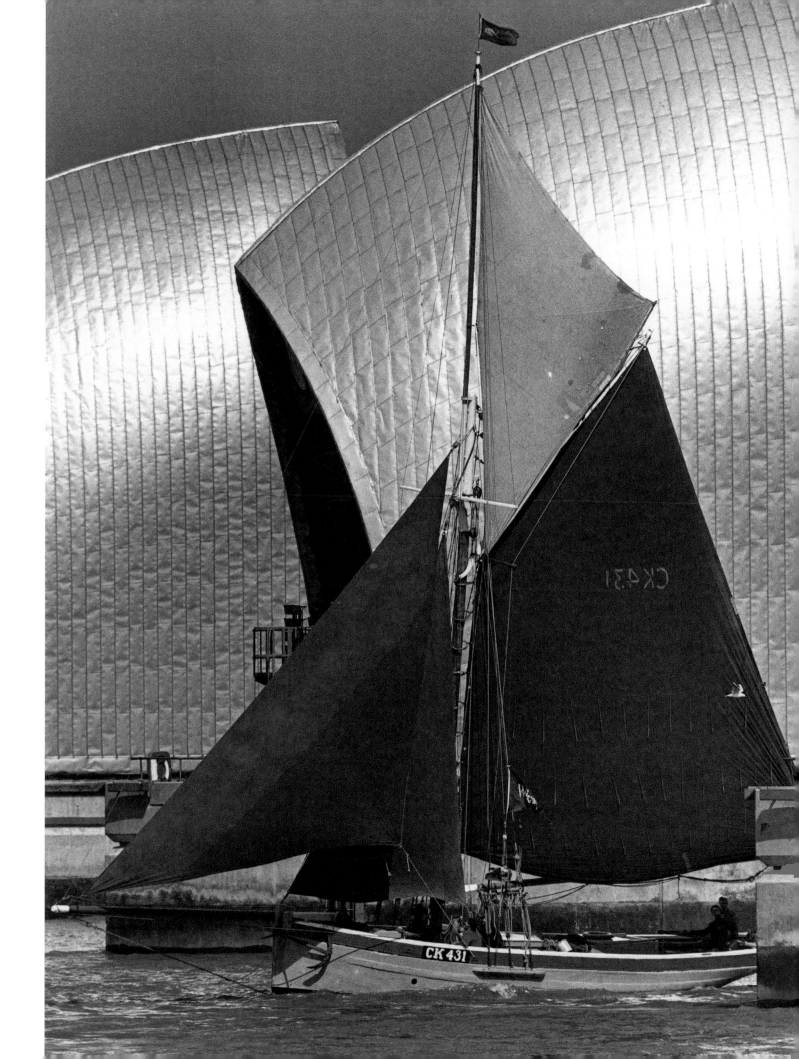

London
at

04

War

above

A machine-gun post in Parliament Square disguised as a W.H. Smith's bookstall. The advertisement for *Truth* comes across as quite Orwellian posted on the side of a building pretending to be something it is not, in a war when press photographs had to be passed by the Ministry of Information Press and Censorship Bureau. 15th March 1942.

opposite

The bombed Chamber of the House of Commons undergoing demolition. 10th July 1945.

THE THAMES IS THE REASON that London grew up where it did, and it has been the lifeblood of the city throughout most of London's history – but during the Second World War the river was almost the downfall of the capital. The meandering course of the Thames, impossible to disguise, guided German bombers towards their targets during their night-time raids, particularly during full-moon periods, known as 'bombers' moons', when the light would glint off the water.

Blitz comes from the German word *blitzkreig*, meaning lightning war, but in fact the night-time air raids were anything but lightning war; they were part of a slow process of attrition intended to demoralise and disable British cities. The Blitz affected all the British towns that were important for war: Belfast, Manchester, Sheffield, Glasgow, Hull, Plymouth and, most viciously, Coventry. But even despite the intensity of the raid on Coventry, the main Blitz was reserved for London, and the night of 7th September 1940, 'Black Saturday', marked the start of 76 consecutive nights of bombing, except for 2nd November when bad weather grounded the Luftwaffe.

But if Hitler had hoped to terrorize the population into surrender the Blitz had the opposite effect, uniting people in their determination to survive. George VI announced that, 'It is not the walls that make up the city, but the people who live within them. The walls of London may be battered, but the spirit of the Londoner stands resolute and undismayed.' After a week in which more than fourteen hundred incendiary devices and almost one thousand tons of high explosives fell on Docklands, Buckingham Palace was bombed by a lone raider on 13th September, prompting Queen Elizabeth (now HM The Queen Mother) to say: 'I'm glad we have been bombed; I feel I can look the East End in the face.'

London expected the worst, and preparations for war included the Evacuation and the implementation of three circles of defence around the capital: two anti-tank lines manned by the Home Guard, the outer one very roughly as far out as the present M25 and the inner one roughly in the position of the north and south circular roads, with an inner line of defence manned by the regular army. This inner line of defence included machine guns mounted on strategic buildings, and pill-boxes disguised as tea kiosks and newsstands.

But none of this was any defence against air raids, and although after 76 nights of terror the raids became more sporadic, they were no less vicious. The most severe bombing raid of the war came on 10th May 1941 when a fleet of 500 German aircraft started more than 2,200 separate fires raging from Romford to Hammersmith and killed 1,436 civilians, more than any other raid on London. The Houses of Parliament were damaged 11 times during the war but on 10th May a high explosive bomb fell near Victoria Tower, bringing tons of rubble crashing down into the Royal Court, with another destroying the House of Commons, causing fires that the Chief Superintendent of the London Fire Brigade described as 'an impenetrable inferno of flames'. On the same night 250,000 books were burned in the British Museum, countless homes were destroyed and Westminster Abbey, the Law Courts, the Royal Mint and the Tower of London were hit by bombs.

above

Mr and Mrs Ray, with two policemen and one of their neighbours, examine a landmine that floated down by parachute and landed in their back garden. Mrs Ray keeps a safe distance from the ton of high explosive, sheltering behind her sturdy garden fence. 27th September 1944.

right

Mrs Pepper smiles cheerfully as she carries on with washing day as if nothing had happened. 19th May 1941.

opposite

Bombed-out residents of Canning Town serve tea made on a primus stove on the street in front of their home. (Not dated.)

It was the morale of ordinary Londoners, not the destruction or otherwise of its landmarks, that would make or break the city, and morale stayed remarkably high. Casualties were fewer than had been feared before the war but the destruction of buildings and homes was immense: the Blitz destroyed or damaged 3.5 million homes in metropolitan London, and a further 1.25 million were damaged by Flying Bomb attacks in 1944–45.

Philosopher Bertrand Russell had predicted that London would be 'levelled to the ground on the outbreak of war', while the Air Ministry feared that one week's bombing would involve 18,750 casualties in the capital. Fortunately the Air Ministry's figures proved inaccurate, with 20,000 dead and 25,000 injured in the period of the main Blitz between September 1940 and May 1941 – a terrifying number but far less than had been feared, at just over twice the number of casualties predicted for a single week. The intensity of the Blitz becomes clear when the number of deaths during those nine months is compared with 29,890 Londoners killed by enemy action during the entire six years of the war, 84 per cent of that total occurring during the Blitz.

Bertrand Russell's predictions about the levelling of the city were also over-estimated, although most of Stepney, Bermondsey and Poplar were laid waste and at least 1.5 million Londoners were made homeless. Some of the lucky ones were able to contemplate the near misses, examining unexploded bombs or landmines in their back gardens; this one (above) in Finsbury Park floated down on a parachute and, although packed with a ton

of high explosive, failed to detonate. Chalked on the case of the mine were the words *Liebe Tommy* – Dear Tommy. Another unexploded bomb that buried itself under St Paul's Cathedral took three days to extricate; it was then driven away on a lorry to Hackney Marshes where it was blown up, leaving a crater 100 feet in diameter.

For others, the best they could do was to hang out the washing on a roof terrace newly created by the Luftwaffe or gather what was left of their belongings in the street, improvising field kitchens and burning bomb-damaged furniture to keep warm. It is remarkable that Londoners managed to look so cheerful in the face of such destruction, perhaps because simply being alive was more important than the bricks and mortar of their homes. Muriel Spark recalls the atmosphere of numbed acceptance in her novel *The Girls of Slender Means*:

> The streets of the cities were lined with buildings in bad repair or no repair at all, bomb-sites piled with stony rubble… the wallpapers of various quite normal rooms would be visible, room above room, exposed, as on a stage, with one wall missing… There was absolutely no point in feeling depressed about the scene; it would have been like feeling depressed about the Grand Canyon or some event of the earth outside everybody's scope.

below
Firemen in action in
Cannon Street, with St
Paul's in the background.
17th April 1941.

below
The result of an
explosion in the
underground concourse
of Bank Station, close to
the Royal Exchange.
January 1941.

As well as people's homes, some nine million square feet of office space was destroyed by the Blitz, much of it within the Square Mile. About one third of the City was completely destroyed and, although this was only just over half the area destroyed by the Great Fire of 1666, rebuilding took much longer than after the Fire – partly because of underground works on transport and utilities, and partly because of a massive amount of replanning.

Christopher Wren had drawn up ambitious plans for the rebuilding of the City after the Great Fire, with Parisian-style boulevards radiating outwards from the Royal Exchange, but these plans were lost in the rush as people took it upon themselves to rebuild their property on the original sites. After the Second World War, however, two reports were produced, laying down planning guidelines for the future of London and, in 1944, an Act of Parliament gave local authorities the right of compulsory purchase over blitzed areas. As a result the City gained 115 acres, including most of the site now occupied by the Barbican Centre.

It is ironic that the Royal Exchange, surrounded by craters, should be carrying a banner exhorting people to Dig For Victory. This campaign for self-sufficiency saw people growing-their-own in bomb-sites and back yards, in temporary allotments, public parks and even in the moat of the Tower of London. The swimming pool of the Ladies Carlton Club in Pall Mall was converted into a giant pigsty, and waitresses at the Quality Inn restaurant on Regent Street grew their own tomatoes in window boxes.

The survival of St Paul's amidst all this destruction was a great morale-booster for Londoners, and the sight of the great cathedral 'like a great ship lifting above the smoke and flames' became a symbol of hope and defiance. Dorothy Barton remembers travelling to work in the City:

> As I turned on to London Bridge I could see St Paul's Cathedral standing alone in an
> area of complete devastation. The air was full of smoke and the smell of burning…
> I felt a lump in my throat because, like so many people, I felt that if St Paul's survived,
> so would we. Halfway across the bridge a group of firemen, with smoke-blackened
> faces and clothes, were rolling up their hoses after battling with the fires all night.

Quite spontaneously the office workers broke into a cheer and several shook hands with the firemen as they passed. In tears I walked along, it was such an emotional moment. I don't think anyone should ever forget that firemen were heroes during the entire war, especially during the Blitz.

opposite top
'London Carries On' –
tube trains are seen
still running under a
crater caused by
German air raids.
22nd April 1941.

opposite bottom
Air raid damage at
St Pancras Station,
quickly repaired by the
London, Midland &
Scottish Railway.
26th August 1942.

above

A London bus in a bomb
crater left by another
night of air raids.
23rd January 1942.

The huge crater outside the Royal Exchange was the result of a bomb that destroyed Bank Station, killing 57 people and causing damage to trains 62 feet below ground. London's transport system was just as much at risk as its buildings and people, and the destruction of buses and stations became commonplace.

Some 166 buses and coaches, 69 trams and 15 trolley buses were destroyed during the war, 65 of the buses in Croydon Garage on a single night: 10th May 1941, the worst night of the Blitz. After the bombing of Coventry the Germans coined a new verb, *coventrieren*, to coventrise, and on 10th May London was coventrised. That Saturday night there were 20 direct hits on London Transport railways, four of its tunnels were breached by bombs and nine tracks were blocked, yet within ten days services had been 'substantially restored' except for a short stretch of the Circle Line between King's Cross and Euston.

On the main line railways it was a similar story, with the railway companies repairing damage and resuming services extremely quickly. Dorothy Barton recalls that 'the trains usually ran on time and

even when the big London terminals were hit during a raid, as they sometimes were, trains were disorganised for only a short while'. The photograph (right) of bomb damage at St Pancras Station was released by the censor only after the London Midland & Scottish Railway had the trains running again, so that the image of destruction would be accompanied by a story of resilience in the face of German attacks. Doris Lawrence remembers being stuck on a train in an air raid on her way to work:

> The train got stopped on the railway bridge going over the river, not a very healthy spot to be in an air-raid… We were there for hours… eventually those who had seats in the train exchanged places with those standing to give them a rest. People got hungry and lunch packets came out and were offered all round the fellow-passengers. There was a great camaraderie amongst people. I got to work at five o'clock, ready to go home at half past five!
>
> At work we never knew which way we would be going home. There might be a direct hit on one of the London stations. Somehow the firm found out and would inform us about half an hour before finishing time. I never asked how they got this information. I never even thought about it.

The Underground was less vulnerable than the main line railways, and provided not only a reliable and relatively safe means of transport but also vital shelter for the public, although at the start of the war this was not officially sanctioned. There were two reasons why the authorities did not want to use the tube system as a public air raid shelter: they wanted to keep the tunnels clear for the movement of troops, the injured and evacuees; and they were worried that, once underground, people would stay there. But they had to back down when within days of the Blitz starting people automatically made their way to the tunnels for shelter. A platform ticket was the only requirement to enter a station and before long there were in excess of 150,000 people camping nightly on platforms, in corridors, and even on the escalators.

By 1943 the authorities had followed the public's lead. Seventy-nine stations were converted into deep shelters, supposedly providing accommodation for 75,000 people, though with only 22,800 bunks. G.W. Stonier confirmed one of the authorities' fears in his *Shaving through the Blitz*: 'The danger here is not bombs, or even burial or typhus, but of going native and not coming up again till after the war, when you will emerge with a large family and speaking another language.'

But for some the danger *was* still bombs, despite the fact that they were deep underground: on 14th October 1940 a direct hit on the northbound station tunnel at Balham burst a water main, killing 60 people sheltering on the platform below and creating a river three feet deep through the station; and in January 1941 a bomb exploded in the underground concourse of Bank Station (*see picture on page 77*) killing 57 people. Despite these incidents the tube provided a relatively safe place to shelter, and the government even took to providing entertainment for the shelterers, through the wartime entertainment organisation ENSA.

below
A mother pretends to sleep for the photographer while her baby lies wide awake beside her in one of the deep-level shelters. 21st July 1944.

above
A bomb crater in
Piccadilly Circus.
8th February 1944.

Meanwhile, above ground, the destruction continued. At Piccadilly the Circus had become a huge crater, though the famous signs survived and 'Eros' had already been evacuated to Egham for the duration, and Oxford Street was filled with rubble and snaking hosepipes instead of shoppers and traffic. The John Lewis department store was so badly damaged by incendiaries in this raid on 18th September 1940 that, although the shell of the building survived, it had to be rebuilt after the war.

Elsewhere in the West End the theatres had been compulsorily closed during the first week of the Blitz. The Windmill was the first to re-open and the only theatre to remain open for the rest of the war, afterwards adopting the proud slogan 'We never closed'. The Café de Paris, which had been advertised as the safest nightclub in town, took a direct hit in March 1941: the club was packed with officers on leave and shattered glass from the mirrored walls, copied from the ballroom of the *Titanic*, added to the carnage.

At Langham Place, Broadcasting House was hit, despite the gleaming Portland stone having been painted battleship grey as a precaution. On the evening of 15th October 1940 a bomb exploded within the building, killing seven people. Listeners heard a muffled blast and a voice reassuring newsreader Bruce Belfrage that it was 'all right', after which he continued to read the *Nine O'Clock News*. Less than two months later a landmine exploded in Portland Place, starting a fire in Broadcasting House that took a full seven hours to put out. The same blast shattered the 38,000 gallon water tank in the Langham Hotel opposite, the tons of water causing more damage than the blast itself.

The West End also had several steel-framed buildings that provided safe shelter for the lucky few while the masses were packed into the tube stations below. The Turkish baths in the basement of the Dorchester Hotel were filled with rows of beds, some reserved for VIPs, while the underground banqueting hall at the Savoy was divided into one part dining hall and one part dormitory – with a separate section for snorers!

above
The aftermath of air
raids on Oxford Street,
with the John Lewis
store in the foreground.
18th September 1940.

As well as disrupting people's shopping in the West End and their work in the City, the Blitz had a devastating affect on children's schooling. Some 690,000 children were evacuated from the capital in September 1939 and most schools were evacuated en masse, teachers and all, to minimise the disruption. But those children who stayed in London left the authorities with a special problem: there were no organised schools, and only 300 teachers remained in the capital.

After the Evacuation the expected air raids did not materialise so many of those who had been evacuated began to return to London. By Christmas 1939 nearly half of all evacuees had returned home but many children found that their schools had been converted for war use as auxiliary fire stations, ambulance stations or rescue service depots. One Brockley schoolgirl remembers that 'the upstairs hall was about half the size it should have been as it had been bombed… we used three classrooms on that floor and one on the ground floor… one part of the school had been taken over by the ambulance service and another was given over to the heavy rescue service'.

Only 120 out of 900 elementary schools reopened, leaving 34,000 London schoolchildren being taught in shifts at school, with a further 100,000 receiving home tuition in small groups. More schools began to reopen during 1940 but in September the Blitz began in earnest and many of them were bombed. Fortunately most of the air raids were at night so the schools were unoccupied but this was not always the case. On 20th January 1943 a 1,100lb bomb fell on Sandhurst Road School in Catford. Teachers had already begun to lead the children down into the shelters but they were too late, and the bomb killed 38 children and 6 teachers. A London County Council nursery school was destroyed at night when it was empty; its pupils and staff were subsequently evacuated to a school in Kent, where it was hit in June 1944 by a flying bomb, killing 22 out of 30 children and 8 of the 11 staff.

More than 200 schools were damaged in the Blitz and 150 completely destroyed, including Single Street School in Stpeney, pictured here. The children returned to their school to play, despite the damage and a playground full of rubble, but the watchman banned them from the school grounds. On 9th June 1942 the children met the Mayor of Stepney to demand the right to use their playground but there is no record of whether their deputation was successful.

But the war was not always bad news for schoolchildren. During exam time some pupils longed for the disruption of the air raid sirens, and one girl said years later that, 'I kept hoping the sirens would go – if they went while we were taking [our exams] they would have accepted our mock marks and I would have passed – but there wasn't a sound.'

above
Pupils of Single Street School in Stepney playing in their bombed-out playground.
9th June 1942.

opposite
Peter Hodgson, of Single Street School in Stepney, who appealed to the Mayor for room to play cricket in the blitzed playground.
9th June 1940.

When victory finally came in 1945 it left the world a changed place. America became, and has since remained, the world's greatest power, and the Iron Curtain went up in Europe, dividing east from west for more than forty years. In Britain the social changes were enormous: the Welfare State and the National Health Service were born out of the upheavals of the war, people's aspirations and expectations changed, the class system was weakened, and women's emancipation took a huge step forward.

In London the immediate changes were less far-reaching but more visible. Street parties and thanksgiving services took place among the rubble, and the city began to put itself back together. Victory in Europe was declared on 8th May 1945, the day after Germany's surrender, and throughout the country people began to celebrate. Street parties were organised using whatever rations were available: many people remember the treat of having jelly, one was delighted to win a packet of tea, and David George remembers a street party in South Ealing: 'They had a street party down the corner from where we live, they brought out all the Morrison shelters and made one long table with them. People knew the end was coming and had been saving up their rations – for the first time in ages we had toffee…'

As well as parties there were the victory thanksgiving services, this one in the true heart of London. City workers filled every seat for a lunch time service in the bombed-out ruins of the Church of St Mary-le-Bow, Cheapside, formerly the home of the famous Bow Bells which were destroyed in the same air raid. St Paul's is framed in what had been a memorial window to John Milton, who was born nearby on Bread Street and educated at St Paul's school. His words from *Paradise Lost* might well describe the experience of Londoners during the war: 'Long is the way and hard, that out of hell leads up to light.'

And although Victory in Japan did not come until August 1945 the lights were going back on in London and the rest of Europe, quite literally. After six years of blackout the streets were being lit again at night, to the fascination of many young children, some of whom had never a streetlight in use.

Green

05

London

LONDON HAS A REMARKABLE NUMBER of parks, thanks mainly to the greed of Henry VIII and the generosity of Victorian philanthropists. There are no fewer than 1,700 public open spaces of more than one acre, covering a total area of 67 square miles, and during the 1960s *The Times* described the city as 'graced with daffodils and anemones, so green with parks and squares that, as the saying goes, you can walk across it on the grass'.

Apart from large areas of ancient common-land, London is also blessed with a number of historic royal parks and several Victorian municipal parks. Much of the land now occupied by the royal parks was taken from the church at the Dissolution of the Monasteries and used by Henry VIII for hunting grounds and deer parks. This confiscated land was laid out as royal parkland and was later, under the Stuarts and the Prince Regent, made available for public enjoyment. The municipal parks were opened by the Victorians as places of education and instruction as well as pleasure, the first being Hackney's Victoria Park in 1842, soon followed by Battersea, Finsbury and Southwark parks.

Although it is named for the Prince Regent (later George IV), Regent's Park, originally part of the vast Forest of Middlesex, is one of the many royal parks appropriated from the church by Henry VIII. He set aside 554 acres as a hunting ground which remained Crown property until Charles I used it as a pledge for gunpowder and weapons with which to fight the Civil War. After his execution, Marylebone Park, as it was then known, was sold at auction; records state that the park included 16,297 trees valued at £1,774 8s 0d. The trees were felled, many of them going to the Navy for ships, and when the park was re-acquired by the Crown after the Restoration most of the land had been ploughed over and was subsequently used as farmland.

The farm leases expired in 1811 and a competition was held to find the best design for a new estate. The competition was won by John Nash, who proposed a continuous belt of elegant terraced

above
The Victorian gardens in Regent's Park shortly after being restored. 18th August 1996.

below
The Regent's Park
annexe of the
Marylebone Public
Library. The library put a
stall in Regent's Park
from which visitors to
the park could borrow
books free on production
of an identity card.
11th August 1942.

right
Skating in Regent's Park.
1929.

houses around the park; the park itself would contain two grand circuses and no less than 56 villas, all to be linked with Westminster by Regent Street. Work stopped in 1826 when the money ran out but the resulting park gives an idea of the 'garden city' that Nash and the Prince Regent had envisaged, an attempt to create the old ideal of *rus in urbe*, the country in the city.

right

Edwardian society
promenading along
Rotten Row in Hyde
Park. The name Rotten
Row is a corruption of
route du roi, or King's
Road. c1902.

Hyde Park takes its name from the Saxon word for 100 acres, although it is now more than three times
that size, and it was bequeathed to the monks at Westminster soon after the Norman Conquest as a
source of meat. The land was taken by Henry VIII at the Dissolution as a royal hunting ground and the
park was opened to the public by James I in the 17th century, when refreshments advertised included
'milk from a red cow'.

After the Civil War the park was sold on the orders of Parliament and subsequently became a
popular place for racing coaches. Diarist John Evelyn records that Cromwell himself indulged in coach
racing and 'provoked the horses [so much] with the whip that they grew unruly' and threw him from his
coach. Worse was to come because, 'his foot getting caught in the tackling, he was carried away a
good while in that posture during which time a pistol went off in his pocket. But at last he got his foot
clear and so came to escape'.

At the Restoration Charles II enclosed Hyde Park with a brick wall, at which time the park became a
fashionable place to be seen; the beau monde would ride around the circular drive known as the Ring,
pausing to gossip and indulge in mutual admiration. Two centuries later it was still popular, and Charles
Dickens the younger describes the scene: 'For two or three hours every afternoon in the season... the
particular section of the drive which happens that year to be "the fashion" is densely thronged with carriages
moving round and round at little more than walking pace, and every now and then coming to a dead-lock.'

By the time Dickens was writing about Hyde Park 'the drive' included Rotten Row, which was created as a bridle path by William III, its name a corruption of *route du roi*, or king's road. When the road was laid out in the late 17th century the park was notorious for highwaymen (one was hanged in 1687 for killing a woman who had swallowed her wedding ring to prevent him from taking it), so William had 300 lanterns hung from the trees along the route, making Rotten Row the first road in England to be lit at night.

The present appearance of the park is mainly thanks to Queen Caroline, consort of George II, who united Hyde Park and Kensington Gardens and in 1730 dammed the Westbourne River in order to form the Serpentine, now the scene of the famous Christmas Day plunge. The lake (known at first as the Serpentine River) was the scene of a miniature re-enactment of the Battle of Trafalgar in 1814, the drowning of Shelley's first wife, Harriet Westbrook, after the poet had eloped with the 16-year-old Mary Wollstonecraft, and was described by Dickens the younger in an 1888 guide as 'a favourite place for skating, and about the most dangerous in London'.

above
The traditional Christmas Day swim in the Serpentine. About twenty members of the Serpentine Swimming Club, aged between 19 and 75, took part in the annual 100-yards race, known as the Peter Pan Cup. 25th December 1998.

above
London's parks provide
something of the country
in the city, but sheep
grazing in St James's
Park is taking Martial's
ideal of *rus in urbe* a
little too literally.
12th May 1939.

Dickens clearly had either an obessession for skating or an excessive concern for people's safety
because in the same guide he describes St James's Park as 'little more than an enclosed garden, nearly
half of which is occupied by a shallow piece of water, probably the safest for skating in London'. Two
centuries earlier Samuel Pepys had been 'over to the Parke, where I first in my life, it being a great
frost, did see people sliding with their skeates, which is a very pretty art'. However, Pepys did not
consider St James's to be as safe as Dickens did: when a fortnight later he accompanied the Duke of
York to the park, Pepys wrote that 'though the ice was broken and dangerous, yet he would go slide
upon his skeates... I did not like it but he slides very well'.

St James's is the oldest of the royal parks, and takes its name from St James's in the Fields, a
hospital for leper women that once stood close by: the park itself was a marshy field where the lepers
fed their hogs. The hospital became a convent but was dissolved in 1532; Henry VIII rebuilt it as St

James's Palace and drained the field for use as a bowling alley and tilt yard, and later as part of a hunting chase. James I had a menagerie and an aviary in the park, pre-empting the fact that in the 21st century St James's is an inner-city wildfowl reserve: the aviary, which was later enlarged by James's grandson Charles II, stood on the south side of the park close to what is now Birdcage Walk.

It was Charles II who opened the park to the public, having extended it by 36 acres and converted several small ponds into the long strip of water known as the Canal. He loved strolling in the park with his mistresses, playing *palla a maglio* there (a ball game that gave its name to Pall Mall) and could often be seen swimming in the Canal. The descendants of two pelicans presented to Charles by the Russian ambassador can still be seen in the park.

The opening of this and other royal parks to the public gave a greater freedom for informal mixing of the monarch and his subjects, which was not always seen as a good thing by later monarchs with a greater desire for privacy. George II's queen, Caroline, who put so much money and time into the landscaping of Hyde Park and Kensington Gardens, asked Sir Robert Walpole what it would cost to close the royal parks to the public. 'Only three *crowns*,' replied Walpole, referring to the crowns of England, Scotland and Ireland.

A desire to close the royal parks seems incompatible with the fact that it was George II and Queen Caroline who first opened Kensington Gardens to the public, although only on Sundays when the court was at Richmond and only to 'respectably dressed people', with the specific exclusion of soldiers, sailors and liveried servants. The Broad Walk soon became as fashionable and as crowded as the Mall had been a century earlier, but Caroline's motivation for wanting to close the parks may have been the fact that George II was robbed in Kensington Gardens early one morning while taking his customary lone walk.

George's great-grandson William IV described to Lord Ducannon how a man 'approached the King, but with great respect, and told him he was in distress, and was compelled to ask him for his money, his watch, and the buckles on his shoes'. The King told this polite robber that there was a seal on the watch chain that was 'of little or no value, but which he wished to have back, and requested he would take it off the chain and [return] it'. The man agreed to have it removed and return it the next day so long as the King told no-one about the incident. Both kept their word and the thief returned the following day with the Royal Seal, presumably not realising its significance.

Kensington Gardens were once the gardens of Kensington Palace, although they are not actually in Kensington: the border with the City of Westminster separates the palace from the Round Pond. Technically the gardens are a separate entity from the adjoining Hyde Park, although it is difficult to notice any change, and the part of the Serpentine that extends into Kensington Gardens is officially known as the Long Water although it is part of the same body of water.

The Round Pond was established by Queen Caroline, working with William Kent, in 1728 (two years before they created the Serpentine) and it has been a popular place of relaxation ever since, referred to by the skating-fixated Dickens as 'that favourite resort of skaters'. In summer the Round Pond became a favourite resort of those wanting to sail model boats, some of the boats being large enough to require a means of transport to get them there: J.M. Barrie, the creator of *Peter Pan*, suggested that the reason so many children were bow-legged was that they 'had to walk too soon because their father needed the perambulator [to bring his boat to the Round Pond]'.

But the popularisation of Kensington Gardens did not go down well with the wife of the Russian ambassador to Victorian England, who commented that the gardens had been 'annexed as a middle-class rendezvous. Good society no longer goes there except to drown itself'. (Presumably she was referring to the drowning of Shelley's first wife, Harriet Westbrook, in the Serpentine, showing that just like most modern visitors, she drew no distinction between Hyde Park and Kensington Gardens.)

A statue of Barrie's *Peter Pan* by Sir George Frampton has stood in Kensington Gardens since 1912, and the swings in the children's playground at the north end of the Broad Walk were donated by Barrie himself. On 30th June 2000 a new playground was opened as a memorial to Diana, Princess of Wales, funded by the Royal Parks Agency and the Diana, Princess of Wales, Memorial Committee. Designed on the theme of Barrie's 1904 play, it has a pirate ship, crocodile, and wigwams in addition to the more traditional playground equipment. Even the toilets and offices follow the theme, being designed as a buried building echoing the 'home underground' of the original story. The curved walls of this buried building were constructed using a technique developed in the engineering of the Sydney Opera House.

opposite
Seagulls inland for the winter join the swans, ducks and pigeons at the Round Pond, Kensington Gardens.
11th November 1971.

above

Narrow boats on the
Grand Union Canal.
19th August 1997.

As well as the various parks, London's 'hidden' green spaces include reservoirs, railway embankments, derelict ground, disused gravel pits and the network of canals, whether in use or not – one of London's newest parks, Burgess Park in Southwark, is built along the line of the old Grand Surrey Canal. The canals make a peaceful adjunct to the city's roads and rail lines; the towpaths are used by walkers, fishers, horse riders and cyclists, while the water itself provides a place for recreation and, for some, a space to live.

But although in modern London the canals provide a quiet oasis from the noise and bustle, they were built as heavy-duty waterways in an industrial age. The Grand Junction Canal from London to the Midlands was begun in the 18th century and was connected to Regent's Canal in 1820; in its first year the Regent's Canal handled 120,000 tons of freight, mainly timber, coal, and ice. However the freight-carrying company folded after claims arising from the Regent's Park Explosion of 1874, when a barge caught fire while passing under the Macclesfield Bridge near the North Gate of Regent's Park. It was carrying the sensible combination of three barrels of petrol and five tons of gunpowder, and

the resulting explosion destroyed the barge, its crew, and the bridge, as well as blowing out house windows up to a mile away.

During the 19th century the ice used by restaurants, markets, butchers and fishmongers to keep food fresh had to be cut by saw from rivers, lakes, ponds and canals, and then stored underground in specially constructed ice wells. As demand grew and London's waterways became more polluted, ice had to be imported, sometimes 350 tons at a time, and was landed at the Limehouse Basin before being transferred to ice wells constructed at various points along the Regent's Canal. The first consignment of ice was imported by William Leftwich but it melted while Customs Officers tried to decide what import duty to charge.

The coming of the railways was the beginning of the end for the industrial use of canals; many were bought up for conversion into railways, and there were various plans put forward between 1845 and 1883 to do just that with the Regent's Canal. Fortunately it survived, and in 1929 became part of the Grand Union Canal. Commercial traffic had ceased by the end of the 1960s but in 1974 councils and local authorities began to open up the towpaths, giving the canal a new lease of life as a public leisure facility, 'a green strip in an urban setting'.

At the smart, western, end of the canal is a leafy triangular basin lined with brightly painted barges and houseboats: Little Venice, a nickname coined by one-time resident Robert Browning who settled there after the death of his wife Elizabeth Barrett Browning and said that the view reminded him of Venice where they had spent many pleasurable days together.

above

Children from Winton School, Islington, at the Camley Street Nature Park shortly before its official opening. 12th May 1985.

Whereas Robert Browning chose to live by the picturesque canalside of the Paddington Basin (now overshadowed by the A40 Westway Flyover), Verlaine and Rimbaud slummed it at Royal College Street close to St Pancras Church, the same church where Shelley first saw Mary Wollstonecraft, who was visiting her mother's grave. The church is now overshadowed by the King's Cross gasometers which have achieved listed status and form an incongruous backdrop to the Camley Street Nature Park. The park, managed by the London Wildlife Trust, features a pond, reed bed, marsh, and willow trees, providing a habitat for birds, butterflies, frogs, newts and toads alongside the canal in what had been an industrial wasteland turned rubbish dump. The Trust was established in 1981 and runs over sixty nature reserves in the capital.

As well as green spaces for wildlife in the capital there are also an increasing number of playgrounds for children; in the photograph opposite youngsters are splashing in the fountain of the children's park at Coram's Fields as part of London Playday, which became a national event in 1991. The aim of the event is to raise awareness of the importance of children's play, for which Coram's Fields is a particularly apt venue: the loggia at the edge of the fields is the last remnant of the 18th-century Foundling Hospital and now forms the border of a purpose-built children's park complete with paddling pool, swings, slides, and animals including hens, horses, sheep, pigs and rabbits. Adults are not allowed to enter unless accompanied by a child.

The Foundling Hospital was set up in 1742 by Thomas Coram, who had been shocked by the number of dead and dying babies abandoned on the streets of London. Unwanted babies could be left anonymously at the hospital and were sent to the country for nursing until they were five; they then returned to the hospital to be educated. The foundation moved to the Home Counties in the 1920s but Thomas Coram would be delighted that the original site was bought by Lord Rothermere and others and preserved as a children's playground.

Hogarth was a patron and Governor of the Foundling Hospital and Handel was another benefactor, donating an organ to the chapel, teaching the choir and giving a performance of *Messiah* that raised £7,000 for the hospital. William Makepeace Thackeray lived close by on Coram Street, the home of one of his characters in *Vanity Fair*, and in *The Ballad of Eliza Davis* he wrote:

> P'raps you know of the foundling Chapel
> Where the little children sing
> Lord I like to hear on Sunday,
> Them there pretty little things.

In 1851, just over a century after Thomas Coram set up the Foundling Hospital, Dr Charles West founded the Hospital for Sick Children at nearby Great Ormond Street. And just as Hogarth and Handel had helped to fund the Foundling Hospital, J.M. Barrie donated the stage, film, television and book rights for *Peter Pan* to the Hospital for Sick Children in 1929.

above
Children splashing in the
Coram's Fields fountain
on London Playday.
22nd August 1990.

The establishment of the Foundling Hospital and the survival of Coram's Fields were both due to the generosity and humanity of a few philanthropic figures, but Hampstead Heath was almost the victim of the opposite: between 1831 and 1871 the Lord of the Manor, Sir Thomas Maryon Wilson, introduced 15 separate parliamentary bills in an attempt to win permission to build on the heath. He wanted to build an estate of 28 villas but only got as far as constructing the bridge across Viaduct Pond, which was intended to carry the access road to the estate and is still known as Wilson's Folly. Sir Thomas owned more than a quarter of the Heath, land which only passed into public ownership after his death in 1871.

Hampstead owes its initial attraction to the discovery in 1698 of chalybeate springs said to be 'of the same nature and equal in virtue with Tunbridge Wells'. The springs are commemorated in street

names such as Well Walk and Flask Walk, although not all of the names are strictly accurate: the Vale of Health was a malarial swamp until the late 18th century. The springs attracted the rich and famous, and as a result Hampstead has more blue plaques than any other London borough but the Heath itself is far more egalitarian in its attractions – too much so for Dickens the younger, who complained 'nor do the donkeys so plentifully provided for the recreation of 'Arry and his young lady add much to the aesthetics of the scene'.

Daniel Defoe was not totally convinced of the attractions of the Heath either, saying that 'it must be confest, 'tis so near heaven, that I dare not say it can be a proper situation, for any but a race of mountaineers, whose lungs have been so used to a rarify'd air, nearer the second region [i.e. heaven], than any ground for 30 miles around it'.

Today Hampstead Heath remains one of London's most popular parks, although locals and regular visitors despise the word 'park': most of the Heath is kept more like a stretch of open countryside than a formal park. The elevation that Defoe complains about results in spectacular views across London, and more than twelve million people a year now visit the Heath to jog, ride horses, fly kites, watch birds, picnic, swim in the ponds, or simply walk across the Heath and admire the view.

The Kit-Kat Club met at Hampstead Heath, the area has been home to artists, actors, composers and politicians, and the list of poets, playwrights and novelists who have lived in the area reads like a literary *Who's Who*. But the resident with perhaps the most abiding literary claim to fame lies in Hampstead Cemetery: Laszlo Bíró, inventor of the ballpoint pen.

below
Football on
Hackney Marshes.
25th September 1983.

Hampstead Heath being, as Defoe pointed out, 'so close to heaven', it commands a great vista south across the Thames flood plain. Being so high the Heath had no problems with drainage, but many of London's other green spaces (and many not so green) had to be reclaimed from the flood plain, which is approximately three miles wide and less than twenty five feet above sea level. Millwall is so named because of the seven windmills that lined the marsh wall and helped drain the low-lying Isle of Dogs. Other land reclaimed from the river includes most of Southwark and Lambeth (which at one time was a tidal marsh under water at every high tide), and the Victoria Embankment, which consists of 37 acres

reclaimed from the Thames by building a wall that extends four metres below the low water mark and
six metres above the high. Much reclaimed land was turned into parks or common land: soil from the
excavation of the Royal Victoria Dock was used to consolidate the marshes of Battersea Fields in order
to create Battersea Park, Hackney Marshes were drained in 1757, and Clapham Marsh was drained
by Christopher Baldwin in 1760 to become Clapham Common.

After it had been drained, Clapham Common was planted and constantly improved until Thackeray
was able to write of it that 'of all the pretty suburbs that still adorn our metropolis there are few that
exceed in charm Clapham Common'. During the 18th and 19th centuries Clapham became surrounded
by the large houses of City merchants and others including Samuel Pepys who, as fellow diarist John
Evelyn records, lived 'in a very noble house and sweate place where he enjoyed the fruit of his labour
in great prosperity'.

Pepys himself records a trip to Hackney, which was a popular Sunday resort: 'With my wife only
to take ayre, it being very warm and pleasant, to Bowe and Old Ford; and thence to Hackney. There
light and played at shuffle-board, eat cream and good cherries; and so with good refreshment home.'

The 337 acres of meadowland that make up the Hackney Marshes stand alongside the River Lea,
up which the Vikings sailed in the 9th century. King Alfred defeated them by diverting the river 'soe
that where shippes before had sayled, now a small boate could scantily rowe', thus running the Vikings
aground. The marshes were drained in the 18th century but were still subject to flooding until the
canal system was built, and were a popular place for hare and rabbit-coursing, fishing, shooting and
bull-baiting. Football and cricket have now replaced shuffleboard and bull-baiting but the Hackney
Marshes are clearly still a popular place for Sunday entertainment.

London

at Play

below
Alfresco eating
'40s-style on Percy
Street. 25th May 1947.

FOR MODERN LONDONERS, AND FOR VISITORS to the city, eating alfresco (from the Italian for 'in the fresh air') is a common enough occurrence when the weather permits but in 1947 it was a newsworthy event. The original caption for the older photograph reads: '"Continental" London. A scene reminiscent of the Continent, showing Londoners eating out of doors at a Percy Street, Tottenham Court Road, restaurant.'

Percy Street lies in Fitzrovia, which has been described as 'a northern extension of Soho', both of which, together with Covent Garden, are now littered with cafés, pubs and restaurants offering alfresco eating and drinking. To describe Percy Street as reminiscent of the continent may be stretching the point, but it is certainly true of Covent Garden – the piazza was based on the Piazza d'Arme in the Italian town of Livorno. And 'Continental' London has been around for longer than many people think;

the Covent Garden piazza was laid out in the 1630s, at which time the square was open and the houses surrounding it were considered extremely fashionable. That all changed with the establishment of the fruit and vegetable market, but when the working market moved to Nine Elms in 1974 Covent Garden reinvented itself as a continental-style piazza, complete with pavement cafés, market stalls, buskers and street entertainers.

In the meantime Covent Garden had been popular with writers and artists, and the same story of riches to writers to reinvention is also true of Fitzrovia and Soho. The name Fitzrovia was coined in the 1930s by the literary group, including Ezra Pound, Dylan Thomas and T.S. Eliot, who used to drink at the *Fitzroy Tavern*. The tavern in turn takes its name from Fitzroy Square, 'one of London's finest squares', which was laid out by the Adam brothers for the great-grandson of the illegitimate son of Charles II, Henry Fitzroy. George Bernard Shaw lived at No. 29 from 1887–98 but by the time Virginia Woolf moved into No. 29 in 1907 (after first checking with the police) her friends considered the area quite disreputable, which is probably what attracted the likes of Dylan Thomas three decades later. However, Fitzrovia now shares the 'raffish, cosmopolitan' reputation of Soho and, perhaps following the lead of this 1947 restaurant, pavement tables abound, particularly on Charlotte Street, which adjoins Percy Street.

Just across Oxford Street is Soho, which takes its name from the huntsmen's cry that echoed through the area when it was a royal hunting ground. Initially built on by princes, dukes and earls, Soho soon changed; as successive waves of immigrants settled in the area the aristocrats moved out and the writers and artists moved in, including Joshua Reynolds, Thomas de Quincey, Wagner, Marx, Verlaine and Rimbaud, and later *Private Eye* and the Groucho Club. Although the porn clubs that gave Soho such a bad name in the 1970s are still in evidence, they exist alongside the media enclave of Wardour Street, the traditional market of Berwick Street, and the gay bars and cafés of Old Compton Street that make Soho the vibrant place that it is today. 'Soho gives you the best and worst of London,' says commentator Rob Humphreys. 'There's nowhere else in the city where such a diverse slice of London comes face to face with each other [sic]: businessmen, clubbers, drunks, theatregoers, fashion victims, market-stallholders, pimps and prostitutes, politicians. Take it all in, and enjoy…'

below
Alfresco eating
'90s-style on Old
Compton Street.
29th July 1994.

right

More than one thousand
schoolchildren recreate
the Cerne Abbas Giant in
front of Kenwood House
to publicise the Heart of
Britain campaign
supporting the Royal
Brompton Hospital.
21st July 1996.

above
Thousands of Londoners
listening to one of the
famous open air concerts
in the natural
amphitheatre to the
south of Kenwood
House. 18th June 1957.

As well as alfresco eating, London provides opportunities for alfresco theatre at the Regent's Park Open Air Theatre and alfresco classical concerts at the Kenwood Bowl, a natural grassy amphitheatre to the south of Kenwood House on Hampstead Heath. The fact that Kenwood House is available for public concerts is thanks to the 1st Earl of Iveagh, head of the Guinness family, who bequeathed the house to the nation in 1927 along with his art collection, including paintings by Rembrandt, Gainsborough, Van Dyck, Reynolds, Vermeer and Franz Hals.

Kenwood's most notorious former owner, the 1st Earl of Mansfield (1705–93), was not quite so public-spirited. Not only was he such an unpopular Attorney-General and Lord Chief Justice that the Gordon rioters nearly razed Kenwood House, but he also denied the public access to 232 acres of Hampstead Heath, including Parliament Hill and Hampstead Ponds. Having sent 102 people to the gallows and sentenced a further 448 to transportation, Mansfield was an obvious target for the Gordon rioters in 'the greatest outburst of civil disobedience in modern British history'. The rioters had already ransacked his Bloomsbury house and were making their way towards Kenwood when they were distracted en route by the landlord of the *Spaniards Inn*, who happened to be an ex-butler of Mansfield's and who gave the rioters free drinks until soldiers arrived to disarm the now-drunken mob; their muskets can still be seen in the saloon bar.

The *Spaniards* has been a tavern since the 16th century and is thought to be named after two Spanish brothers who were joint proprietors and who killed each other in a duel over a woman. Another theory is that it was named after the Spanish ambassador to James II, who lived nearby, but that is far less romantic and would in any case require an apostrophe. The inn is rich in history; Dick Turpin stabled his horse, Black Bess, in the toll house opposite, and is thought to have used the inn as a vantage point for targetting the best coaches leaving London; it was patronised by Shelley, Keats and Byron, and Mrs Bardell and her friends plotted the downfall of Mr Pickwick here in Charles Dickens's *Pickwick Papers*.

below
A City pub selling poultry
as well as pints. 1923.

opposite top
Charwomen enjoying a
quick half in a Vauxhall
pub. May 1951.

opposite bottom
Having a jolly old time at
the *Green Man* in
Bethnal Green. 1950.

The *Spaniards* is an example of that most British of institutions, the pub. Whether referred to as an inn, tavern, hostelry, public house or boozer, the pub, which has its origins in the wayfarers' hostelries and coaching inns of days gone by, often became the focus for an entire community. London's literature, legends, landmarks and traffic reports centre on its pubs, from those immortalised by Charles Dickens to the '*Sun in the Sands* roundabout' which, along with 'Hangar Lane Gyratory' and 'Sheer Weight of Traffic', is one of the the most over-used phrases on the airwaves.

London, and the Monopoly board, would not be the same without the *Angel*, Islington despite the fact that the *Angel* was not actually in Islington. The inn, which was the nearest staging post to London, found itself outside the parish boundary after Islington refused to bury a pauper found on the corner of what is now Liverpool Road; Clerkenwell, having buried the man, claimed *Angel* corner as their own and the parish boundary has run down the centre of the road ever since, separating the *Angel* from Islington by more than just a comma. The inn was rebuilt twice, closed in 1960 and

reopened as a bank in 1982 – the opposite fate to that of *The Counting House* in Cornhill, which was once a bank, and the *Old Bank of England* on Fleet Street, once the Law Courts' branch of the eponymous bank, the former banking hall of which is now renowned as 'a magnificently opulent ale and pie pub'.

Other London pubs are notable for their architects: *The Engineers* in Primrose Hill was designed by Isambard Kingdom Brunel in 1841, and *Ye Olde Watling* on Watling Street, EC1, by Sir Christopher Wren in 1668 as an inn for workmen rebuilding St Paul's after the Great Fire. Realising the importance of pubs to his masons, Wren also designed the original *Old Bell Tavern* on Fleet Street in 1678 for those rebuilding St Bride's Church after the Fire.

The Blind Beggar on Whitechapel Road has its place in London folklore being the pub where Ronnie Kray shot George Cornell, as does the *Ten Bells* on Commercial Street, Spitalfields, as the pub near to which Jack the Ripper's first victim was found, while *Crocker's Folly* in Maida Vale was built as a railway inn opposite the proposed site of Marylebone Station by Frank Crocker, who threw himself off the roof when he discovered that an alternative site had been chosen.

Another institution affected by the building of Marylebone Station, though not as tragically, was Lord's cricket ground. Lord's is the world's most famous cricket ground and the home of the MCC, the Ashes, and a stuffed sparrow that was 'bowled out' by Jehangir Khan in 1936. Looking at the immaculate pitch today it is hard to believe that in the early days the grass was kept short by sheep, which were penned up on match days.

Yorkshireman Thomas Lord first opened a cricket ground in 1787 in Dorset Fields (now Dorset Square, Marylebone), where he was instrumental in setting up the Marylebone Cricket Club, better known as the MCC. In 1811, in anticipation of an increase in ground rent, Lord's relocated to North Bank, St John's Wood, but three years later had to move again when the MCC discovered that the Regent's Canal was to cut across the playing area.

below
Edwardian cricket
supporters looking very
formal at the Oval.
c1905.

Eighty-five years later, in 1899, Lord's almost had to move yet again when the Manchester, Sheffield & Lincolnshire Railway decided to extend its operations into London, change its name to the Great Central Railway, and build Marylebone Station. After a protracted battle Lord's stayed put and the MCC acquired extra land from the railway company in exchange for allowing them to tunnel under the practice ground.

Vying for the title of London's most famous cricket ground, having been the venue of the first ever Test Match between England and Australia, is the Oval, home of the Surrey County Cricket Club. England Captain Nasser Hussain rates the Oval as his favourite place in London, saying that it is 'a special ground for me – England are usually blessed with full houses when we play there, the pitch is one of the best in the country and it's a place where we have often done well in the past'.

Traditionally the Oval stages the last match of any full Test series in England and is now firmly associated with cricket, but things might have been different: towards the end of the 19th century C.W. Alcock was Secretary of both the Football Association and the Surrey County Cricket Club, and the first ever F.A. Cup final was played at the Oval in 1872, when Wanderers beat the Royal Engineers 1–0 in front of a crowd of 2,000. Most of the F.A. Cup finals between 1872 and 1892 were played at the Oval before moving to Crystal Palace and then Wembley Stadium.

opposite top
No prizes for guessing
which team this happy
trio supports.
(Not dated.)

opposite bottom
You'll never walk alone...
A lonely stroll towards
Wembley's famous twin
towers. February 2001.

Wembley Stadium, or the Empire Stadium, Wembley, to give it its full title, was built for the British Empire Exhibition of 1924–25 and completed in time for the 1923 F.A. Cup Final, in which Bolton beat West Ham – no doubt Hammers fans on the day did not look as cheerful as the three pictured opposite. England won the World Cup at Wembley in 1966 and the 'venue of legends' is still thought of as the spiritual home of English football. Perhaps the fact that the stadium closed for redevelopment at the turn of the millennium is a signal that English football should do the same.

Association football, like rugby football, developed out of a much older game that often involved entire villages competing against each other to propel a ball by whatever means possible to one or other village from a point somewhere in between the two. This game evolved and was eventually formalised with the founding of the Football Association at the *Freemasons' Tavern*, London, in 1863, when handling the ball was outlawed. Some football clubs, including Richmond and Blackheath, disagreed with the new rules and stuck with the handling game, forming the Rugby Football Union eight years later in 1871, again in London, at the Pall Mall restaurant; rugby and soccer (which is a corruption of the word 'association') were divided for ever. Dickens the younger describes the situation in 1888:

Both the Rugby Football Union and the Football Association have their head-quarters in London. The Union is the stronger body, and under its laws, which permit the ball being carried, quite five times as many matches are played as under the Association laws, which do not allow of the ball being run with. (To the lay mind it is probable that the Association game would be more likely to answer to the idea conveyed by

above
Scotland fans relaxing
quietly in Trafalgar
Square before the game.
1st June 1983.

116 **LONDON AT PLAY**

the word *foot*-ball. The Rugby game is excellent in its way, but the hand has as much to do with the business as the foot.)... The most important scenes of action are Kennington Oval – where the international matches are played in February and March – Battersea-pk, Blackheath, Richmond, Wimbledon, Wormwood Scrubs and Woolwich.

The Woolwich team, formed in 1886, was named Arsenal after the Royal Arsenal at Woolwich but gave up its south London roots in 1913 when the club moved to Highbury. Three years earlier, in 1910, Millwall Football Club had moved in the opposite direction, relocating south of the river: the club is thought to have originated in the factory team of Morton's canned foods, which was based at Millwall on the Isle of Dogs. Another geographically challenged club is Chelsea, whose ground is actually in Fulham, while Craven Cottage, the home of the other Fulham club, has become 'a sanctuary' for its Chairman Mohamed Al Fayed, who says that 'arriving in London almost thirty years ago, Craven Cottage was one of the first places I went to. Since then Fulham has become part of my life, my blood, my body'. Better hope they don't get relegated, then.

right

The best seat in the house. Jeff Oliver's BBC camera overlooks the courts from 202 feet above Wimbledon. 26th June 1994.

Most of the places listed by Dickens as important for football are now associated with other things: cricket, peace pagodas, and prisons, while Woolwich has its ferry and Wimbledon has the tennis (Wimbledon football club now plays its home games at Crystal Palace). But just as the Oval might have become the home of football, so Lord's almost became the home of tennis, which would have left Wimbledon with…croquet.

The All England Lawn Tennis and Croquet Club, which stages the world-famous Wimbledon Championships, was originally founded in 1868 as the All England Croquet Club, and tennis was not introduced until seven years later. Two years after that, in 1877, the club changed its name to the All England Croquet and Lawn Tennis Club and instituted the first Lawn Tennis Championship. Only a few hundred people watched the first championship, with an audience of 200 paying a shilling each to watch the final. Since then the championship has grown into an event with an attendance of over 375,000 and a media audience of millions throughout the world – and the prices have gone up.

Lawn tennis was introduced by Major Walter Clopton Wingfield, who called his game 'Sphairistike', a name which, not surprisingly, did not stick. The original rules for lawn tennis were drawn up by the MCC at Lord's but the Wimbledon club introduced new rules for its 1877 championship, and the game has been administered by the All England Club ever since. By 1882 croquet was no longer played at Wimbledon so the word was dropped from the club's title but it was restored 'for sentimental reasons' in 1899, albeit as an adjunct to tennis, giving the club its present title.

Apart from tennis, the Wimbledon Championships are also famous for inclement weather and for strawberries and cream. According to the All England Club, 27,000 kilos of strawberries and 7,000 litres of cream are consumed there during Championships Fortnight, but that is not all: tennis fans also make their way through 12,000 kilos of salmon, 30,000 portions of fish and chips, 22,000 slices of pizza, 80,000 half pints of Pimm's, 90,000 pints of beer and lager, and 12,500 bottles of champagne, all of which makes the use of a mere 42,600 tennis balls pale into insignificance.

below
The Spanish horse
troupe El Caballo de
España showing off their
horsemanship at the
Broadgate Arena.
27th July 1994.

Although Virginia Woolf described Wimbledon as 'a dreary, high, bleak, windy suburb on the edge of a threadbare heath', the green spaces of Wimbledon Common surrounding the All England Club make it an apt place for tennis, Pimm's, and strawberries and cream. In contrast, one of London's more surprising venues for fun and games nestles among the office buildings of the City: the Broadgate arena, part of the massive Broadgate complex, is used as an open-air ice rink in the winter and a performance space in the summer.

The Broadgate complex is one of the more successful office developments to have come out of the City's 1980s' spending spree, replacing the old Broad Street Station and incorporating platforms 11–18 of Liverpool Street Station. John Betjeman called Liverpool Street 'the most picturesque and interesting of the London termini' but its two-part development made it confusing and awkward for travellers to use because the last eight platforms, which were added in 1894, almost twenty years after the first part of the station was completed, were shorter than the first ten, creating a barrier between the two halves of the station.

The layout of the station was rationalized as part of the 1985–91 development – the uptake of new office space was much quicker than at Canary Wharf, the traffic-free piazzas proved popular with City workers, and the whole development won critical acclaim; and yet, despite all this success, the developers still went bankrupt.

Modern commentator Iain Sinclair uses Broadgate Circus as an example of his notion that the City has three Dantesque zones, the most accessible of which is 'the interzone – which is neither office nor street. The zone where everything is permitted that is not forbidden. The zone that has no interior and no exterior, where anyone can pause, and no one is at home. Broadgate Circus, with its borrowed amphitheatre, its cod New York ice rink, its cafés and bookshop, its upended Richard Serra girders, is the most visible exemplar of this mood'.

below
The 'cod New York ice
rink' at the Broadgate
complex.
2nd January 1992.

below
The Queen's Silver
Jubilee. An East End
market stall stocked up
in readiness for the
celebrations.
27th May 1977.

As the home of the royal family, London has always had a special place in the celebration of jubilees and coronations, as evinced by the memorabilia on this East End market stall which seems to equate London's landmarks with the monarchy. The idea of celebrating the monarch's jubilee began in the long reign of George III and was continued by Queen Victoria. Jubilee in its original sense meant a 50-year celebration, and the idea of a silver jubilee was not introduced until 1935 during the reign of George V, whose advisers were hoping to repeat the success of Queen Victoria's Golden and Diamond Jubilee celebrations.

For Queen Victoria's Golden Jubilee all the gold and silver coins in the currency were redesigned with a new protrait of the Queen, there was a thanksgiving service at Westminster Abbey and more than thirty foreign royals and the governors of all Britain's colonies and dominions came to pay homage; Victoria wrote afterwards that '*all* was the most perfect success'. By the time of her Diamond Jubilee she had surpassed George III as Britain's longest reigning monarch and the celebrations included a service outside St Paul's Cathedral; this time the Queen wrote that 'the cheering was quite deafening and every face seemed to be filled with real joy. I was much moved and gratified'.

George V's Silver Jubilee was a less formal affair and included street parties, jubilee mugs and a thanksgiving service at St Paul's, after which the King wrote that there were 'the greatest number of people in the streets that I have ever seen'.

Queen Elizabeth II's Silver Jubilee in 1977 followed a similar pattern but it was a much more lavish affair. The February anniversary of her accession was celebrated in church services

across the country during that month but the real celebrations were saved for the summer. The Queen decided that she wanted to share the occasion with as many of her subjects as possible and in three months she made six jubilee tours in the UK and Northern Ireland, covering 36 counties, as well as overseas tours to Western Samoa, Australia, New Zealand, Tonga, Fiji, Tasmania, Papua New Guinea, Canada and the West Indies. It is estimated that she travelled more than fifty-six thousand miles in her jubilee year.

The London week of the Queen's jubilee tours included a Thames river pageant and a State procession to St Paul's watched by an estimated 500 million people around the world. Street parties were held throughout the nation, with more than four thousand reported in London alone; the capital also showed its respect by renaming the London Underground's proposed Fleet Line as the Jubilee Line, and creating a 12-mile Silver Jubilee Walkway around the centre of London, incorporating over 400 aluminium discs set into the pavement.

During the Silver Jubilee more than 100,000 congratulatory cards were received at the palace, but it was not all one-way traffic: 30,000 jubilee medals were distributed and a special 25 pence coin was minted. Some 37,453,000 copper-nickel coins were issued, now worth about £1 each, and 473,000 in sterling silver, which are now worth about £12 each.

London
at

07

Work

THESE RAUCOUS, COLOURFUL SCENES FROM the trading floor of the London International Financial Futures and Options Exchange (LIFFE) may seem to epitomise life in the modern City of London but, although any mention of the Square Mile immediately calls to mind the world of finance, banking and insurance, the Livery Companies and street names of the City are a reminder that finance is only part of the picture, and a relative newcomer at that. Through the ages an enormous variety of trades have flourished within the City walls, and their history, roots and traditions are entwined with those of the City itself.

Among the City Livery Companies are the Apothecaries' Society, which broke away from the Grocers' Company in 1617, the Paviors' Company whose duties, in addition to building pavements, included the removal of scavenging pigs from the streets, the Girdlers' Company, which still presents a girdle to the Sovereign at the Coronation, the Cordwainers' Company, the Tallow Chandlers' Company, and even the Makers of Playing Cards' Company.

Street names evocative of the work carried out there or the goods sold there include Poultry, Pudding Lane, Silk Street, Bread Street, Milk Street, Shoe Lane and Candlewick Street, which was long ago renamed Cannon Street after the candle makers were expelled because of complaints about the smell they caused. Even the church of St Michael Paternoster Royal reflects a City trade: it has no royal connection but is named 'Royal' as a corruption of 'Reole', once a nearby street inhabited by vintners who imported wine from La Reole near Bordeaux.

But despite all this history there is no doubt that today the City's prime function is as a financial centre, at which it excels, dominating Europe in share dealing and foreign exchange, leading the world in futures and options (seen here), and remaining part of a global triumvirate of money markets along with New York and Tokyo.

The City's status as a centre of world commerce was officially recognised in 1570 when Elizabeth I opened Thomas Gresham's mercantile exchange, a continental-style Bourse, or open trading floor, giving it the title by which its successors have been known ever since: the Royal Exchange. During the 18th century the Royal Exchange spawned the London Stock Exchange and the Baltic Exchange, and since then other exchanges have opened, dealing in all kinds of commodities.

above
The trading floor of the London International Financial Futures and Options Exchange (LIFFE). (Not dated.)

opposite
Open-outcry trading at LIFFE. 4th March 1993.

above

A Smithfield meat porter nearly knocks his colleague over with a leg of beef. The bummarees, as the porters are known, were in dispute with retail butchers over the exclusive right to carry meat within the market, seen by the butchers as restrictive practice. 11th February 1956.

opposite

A pork butcher at the busy Smithfield Market keeps his head while all around are losing theirs. 8th April 1993.

Trading in futures means buying and selling commodities that don't physically exist but elsewhere in the City the trading is red in tooth and claw. Smithfield Market was described in the Middle Ages as being 'a plain, grassy space just outside the City walls', and its name is a corruption of 'smooth field'. The cattle market was established by Royal Charter in 1638 but trouble was to follow because during the next century the City expanded, with the result that the market, instead of being just outside the City walls was now just within them. By the beginning of the 18th century there were complaints about unruly drovers deliberately stampeding cattle for fun on their way to market – the distressed animals often took refuge in shops and houses, which is thought to be the origin of the phrase 'a bull in a china shop'.

Charles Dickens describes 19th-century Smithfield in *Oliver Twist*:

> The ground was covered, nearly ankle-deep, in filth and mire; a thick steam perpetually rising from the reeking bodies of the cattle, and mingling with the fog… the unwashed, unshaven, squalid and dirty figures constantly running to and fro… rendered it a stunning and bewildering scene, which quite confounded the senses.

It wasn't until 1855 that the market for live cattle was moved to Islington, and from 1851–66 a new covered market hall was built at Smithfield by Sir Horace Jones, the architect of Tower Bridge. This new market opened in 1868 as the London Central Meat Market and was later extended to form the buildings that stand today, with the exception of the poultry section which burnt to the ground in 1958 and was rebuilt five years later. The market has its own police force and its own licensing hours: from 6.30 a.m. market traders can buy breakfast and an early morning pint.

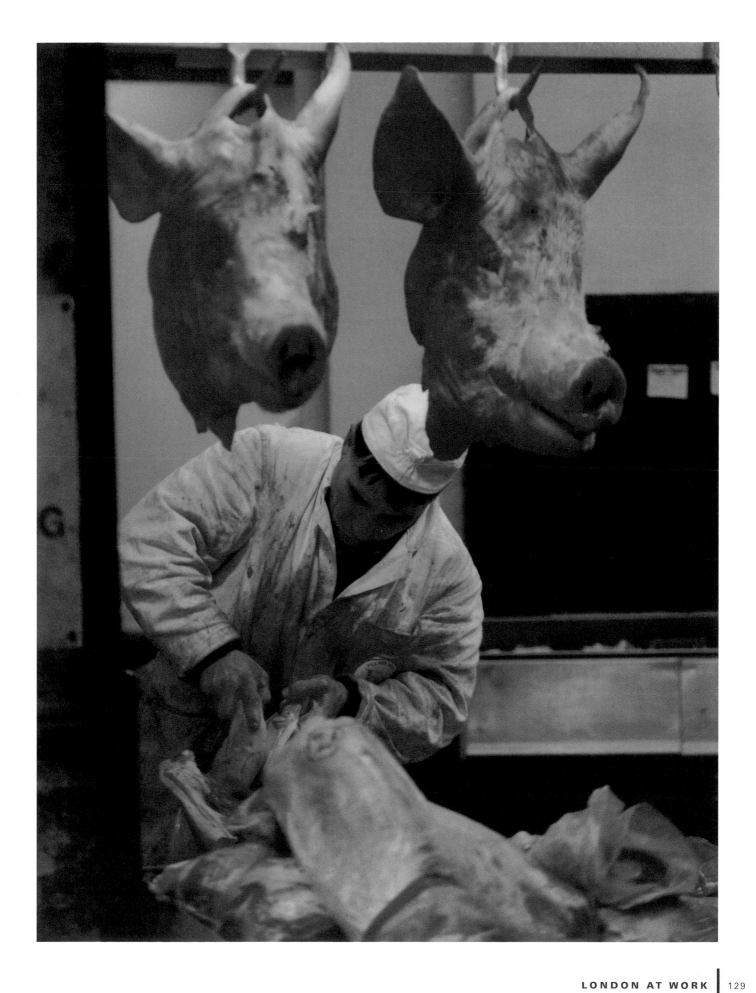

opposite
This porter has a good
head for the fruit and
veg business.
Spitalfields Market was
established in 1682
under licence from
Charles II, bought by

one-time porter Robert
Horner in 1856 and sold
to the City of London
Corporation in 1920. In
1991 the market moved
to Waltham Forest.
14th September 1973.

The origin of the word 'bummaree' (previous page) is uncertain but it was used first to describe porters at Billingsgate fish market, giving rise to the suggestion that it is a corruption of the French *bonne marée*, meaning good, fresh sea fish.

Billingsgate Market dates from the 11th century, at which time it sold various types of goods. It became 'a free and open market for all sorts of fish' by an Act of Parliament in 1698 but 150 years later it was still made up of a random collection of wooden shed buildings. A market hall was purpose-built during the 1850s but quickly proved inadequate, so Horace Jones, who was City Architect to the Corporation of London, was called in to design a new one. It was begun in 1874, just eight years after he had completed the new market hall at Smithfield, and was opened by the Lord Mayor in 1877.

Despite the eminence of Jones's hall, now a Grade II listed building, the site of the market was unworkable. The streets outside were often crammed four deep with carts waiting to be loaded and in 1883 it was reported that 'the deficiencies of Billingsgate and its surrounds are a great scandal to London', and yet it was to be another 99 years before the fish market was moved to New Billingsgate Market, which opened on 19th January 1982 at a 13.5-acre, £11 million-site on the Isle of Dogs. The cost of the new site was amply covered by the sale of Horace Jones's market hall for £22 million.

Porters at the old Billingsgate Market, as well as being the putative source of the title 'bummaree', were distinguished by the flat leather 'bobbing hats' they wore to protect them from the towers of baskets they carried on their heads. The hats were said to be modelled on the leather helmets worn by the archers at Agincourt and were so-named because of the bobbing motion of the baskets as the porters carried them from wholesaler to retailer. New Billingsgate is somewhat less romantic but no doubt less painful for its porters, with fork lift trucks used for all the heavy lifting.

above
The cold storage vaults
under Billingsgate
market in need of a bit of
defrosting.
31st March 1980.

Markets such as Spitalfields, Billingsgate, and Smithfield catered mainly for the wholesale trade in fruit and vegetables, fish, and meat respectively, while ordinary people would be more likely to buy their goods from their local shop or, in the days when they were a more common sight, from a street stall; this one is selling best quality fresh oysters at 3d per half dozen in 1912.

Street vendors have plied their trade in London for almost as long as the Livery Companies, the word 'coster' appearing in manuscripts from as early as the 13th century. 'Costermonger' is defined by Brewer as 'a seller of eatables about the streets' and originates from the sellers of costard apples ('coster' from the apple and 'monger' meaning trader). It is often abbreviated to 'coster' and is so closely associated with the working side of London life that it is 'often applied generically to a Cockney of the East End'.

The definition soon widened from the sellers of apples, first to include the vendors of eatables that included hot eels, pickled whelks, sheep's trotters, hot wine, ginger beer and asses' milk, and then further to include the sellers of wares including matches, sheets of ballads, rat poison, larks, sparrows, nightingales and squirrels. The coster equivalent of the City Livery Companies was the system of 'royalty' that led to the establishment of the Pearly Kings and Queens (see *London Icons, page 36*).

below
Fred Cooke's eel and pie
shop on Kingsland Road,
Hackney, established in
1862 and now the
Shanghai restaurant.
3rd February 1994.

Immediately prior to the First World War oysters were still popular and cheap enough to be sold from a barrow outside a railway station rather than in oyster bars catering for City high-fliers – although in 1861 prices were described as 'very high' when they reached the equivalent of 5p a pint. In the 19th century oysters were a staple working-class food but, like gin, were adopted by the moneyed middle-classes when their rising price made them more exclusive.

As well as for its costers, the East End is legendary for its consumption of eels, although it is not a diet exclusive to London; eels were a staple part of the Saxon diet across the whole of southern England, and the city of Ely actually takes its name from the fact that so many eels were caught on the fens there. (The name is a corruption of El-ge, meaning eel district, as recorded by the Venerable Bede in the 8th century.)

The reason eels are so much a part of the cockney ethos may be due to the influence of Shakespeare, for *Lear*'s Fool instructs his king: 'Cry to it, nuncle, as the cockney did to the eels when she put 'em i' the paste alive.' But in Shakespeare's day the word cockney had a dual meaning, being used both for a Londoner and for an affected cook, so he may not have been deliberately linking Londoners with a love of live eels. He was, however, referring to a delicacy beloved of Henry VIII: eel pie (the 'paste' referred to means pastry). This delicacy is remembered in one of London's strangest place names – each year King Henry would order the first pies of the season to be dispatched to Hampton Court Palace from Eel Pie Island. The tavern on Eel Pie Island was still famous for its pies in the 19th century when, in *Nicholas Nickleby*, Charles Dickens described the beer, shrimps, eel pies and dancing to be had there.

Another occupation forever associated with London due to its literary connections is that of the flower-girl, immortalised by the character of Eliza Doolittle in Shaw's *Pygmalion* and popularised, to his horror, in the musical *My Fair Lady*. The title of Shaw's play is taken from the name of a Cypriot king who fell in love with a statue that he had sculpted of a beautiful woman; Pygmalion prayed to Aphrodite, the goddess of love, and the statue was given life.

However there was no divine intervention for the flower-girls, who were gradually edged out of the market for cut flowers by the growing number of florists' shops. These shops were catering for a new middle-class market for cut flowers, encouraged by *The Gardener's Chronicle*, and Covent Garden Market opened a new Floral Hall in 1886 to cater for the increased trade. Despite this competition, flower-girls were still a common sight on London's streets in 1912 (right), the year that *Pygmalion* was first performed, and these three toothsome smiles are from flower-girls (perhaps the same ones!) celebrating the renewal of their licence in 1931. By the end of the Second World War the trade had all

but disappeared, although their modern descendants can be seen in the hawkers who wait at traffic lights to sell roses to frustrated motorists.

The new flower-market at Covent Garden soon grew to match the turnover of the fruit and vegetable trade, which began 200 years earlier during the 17th century. Modern visitors to London may think of the piazza as a place of street entertainment, craft stalls and expensive cafés but it was a working market until 1974 when the traders relocated to Nine Elms in Battersea – Miss Eleanor Baillie is seen here standing amongst the rubbish after the last day of trading at Covent Garden before the move to Nine Elms. She first visited the market more than sixty years earlier, at about the time the Edwardian flower girls in the picture above were plying their trade.

Covent Garden is so-called because it was originally a garden belonging to a convent, and Long Acre was a long, narrow acre of market gardens belonging to the Abbey of St Peter (now Westminster Abbey). After the Dissolution of the Monasteries the land was granted to the Earl of Bedford, and it was the 5th Earl who in 1670 was granted a royal charter by Charles II to hold a market at Covent Garden. The market soon outgrew itself and from the 18th century onwards suggestions were put forward for a new location but it was to be the late 20th century before the market eventually moved to its new 64-acre site. At its peak the market employed 1,000 porters, and the bustle and colour of Covent Garden were legendary. Charles Dickens the younger wrote that: 'No visitor to London should miss paying at least two visits to Covent Garden: one, say at 6 a.m., to see the vegetable market; the other, later on, to see the fruits and the flowers... the wall-like regularity with which cabbages, cauliflowers, and turnips are built up to a height of some 12 feet is nothing short of marvellous.'

above left
Flower girls with their baskets of cut flowers, once a familiar sight on the streets of London. c1912.

above
The end of an era – Miss Eleanor Baillie looking forlorn as she stands amongst the rubbish with a plant and a bunch of flowers after the last day of trading at Covent Garden Market before the move to Nine Elms. 8th November 1974.

Where there was a wall-like regularity of vegetables (previous page) there was sure to be a delivery man, and where there was a delivery man there was sure to be a whip-lady. But the whip-ladies of pre-First World War Covent Garden were very different from the whip-ladies of post-Second World War Soho. The job of the original whip-ladies was to mind carters' whips while they made deliveries to the market in their horse-drawn wagons, a tradition that was killed off by the arrival of the internal combustion engine. The last thing white-van-man is likely to do while he makes his delivery is hand over his keys to a stranger waiting at the side of the road.

The flower-girls on the previous page had plenty to smile about but not these three chorus girls having a melancholy cup of tea in the canteen of the Windmill Theatre. It is October 1964 and they have just heard that the theatre is to close down.

The Windmill Theatre stands on Great Windmill Street which, although it is hard to believe amidst the roar of modern traffic, takes its name from a windmill that stood there until the late 18th century. The theatre was built in 1910 as a small cinema called the Palais de Luxe but it was unable to compete with the bigger cinemas and re-opened in 1931 as a theatre, finding its fame with the introduction of 'revuedeville' from France, a precursor of the Raymond Revuebar. The theatre quickly became famous for its chorus line and for its risqué revue, although the (almost) naked girls of the revue had to stand motionless to comply with the laws of the time.

Apart from 12 days of compulsory closure in September 1939, the Windmill was the only London theatre to remain open throughout the war, and adopted the proud boast 'We never closed'. However, things came full circle in 1964 when the theatre was closed and rebuilt to fulfil its original rôle as a cinema. The lease was bought in 1973 by none other than Paul Raymond, who presented 'nude entertainment' there until 1981, a far cry from the chorus girls of the 1960s.

Close to Great Windmill Street is Berwick Street market, a down-to-earth fruit and vegetable market in the heart of Soho, looking somewhat incongruous so close to the sleazy neon and the peep shows. The market stretches down into Rupert Street, where clothes, records and CDs take over from the more traditional fruit and veg.

London is renowned for its street markets, which give a feel of what the capital was like when it was still a collection of self-contained communities. Some are well-established, with regular stalls or market buildings, while others, like the bookstalls of Farringdon Road, Charing Cross, and Kingsland Road, are simply tables set up at the side of the road.

Brick Lane and Petticoat Lane are the best-known of 'the seething street markets of the East End', the latter having more than a thousand stalls on a Sunday. The street was originally called Hog's Lane but is shown on a 1608 map as 'Peticote Lane', derived from the old clothes market that had evolved there. Huguenot refugees moved into the area in the 17th century and, being excellent weavers and textile merchants (the Courtauld family is one of the most successful), consolidated the street's connection with clothes and fabrics, including petticoats. In 1830, in an attempt to avoid the unseemly

mention of ladies' underwear, the authorities renamed the street Middlesex Street, still its official title, but the original name has stuck.

Petticoat Lane was one of the largest and busiest of the Victorian street markets, and grew even larger in the 1900s when the street was widened. Several attempts were made to stop the Sunday trading and it was only formally legalised by parliament in 1936. Since then the market has continued to flourish, and has now grown so large that it almost joins nearby Brick Lane market, which is generally considered to be 'more authentically East End' than Petticoat Lane.

Elsewhere street markets also thrive, with the mile-long Portobello Road market, trendy Camden and the picturesque Columbia Road flower market. Bargains are also to be had at 'arty-crafty' Greenwich with its 'not-quite-antiques', at the 'hippy village' of Gabriel's Wharf, at the New Caledonian market in Bermondsey, seen here in 1993 selling silverware, paintings and furniture, and at Borough market, still trading under its Victorian wrought-iron shed.

Commentator Iain Sinclair gives a modern spin to bookstalls like this one in Farringdon Road: 'At the next turning north is a young man with a barrow of paperbacks, trying to make a go of an all-weather bibliothèque… he is forced to share the responsibility for adult literacy in the area with the Oxfam superstore and other less reliable charity bunkers… the barrow is a canvas-covered cousin to the mobile libraries that still ply their trade in remote rural areas.'

above
An art stall in Bermondsey Market, also known as the New Caledonian Market. 19th March 1993.

For those who prefer not to buy their art from a barrow or a market stall there's always the Royal Academy Summer Exhibition, a strange event that appears on the B-list of upper-middle class summer social events in the shadow of Henley, Ascot and Wimbledon, and shares with those events the ubiquitous Pimm's bar.

Anyone, regardless of their skill or experience, may enter paintings for the exhibition; the paintings are viewed by a selection committee and the winners are then hung cheek by jowl in the Academy and sold, usually to the derision of the critics and the dissatisfaction of the entrants. One artist, presumably one of the unsuccessful 90 per cent, wrote this verse in 1875. If his painting was as bad as his poetry there was no wonder his effort wasn't chosen although, as the photographs show, his assessment of the selection process was quite accurate.

> The toil of months, experience of years,
> Before the dreaded council now appears
> It's left their view as soon as in it,
> They down them at the rate of three
> a minute.

The same selection system was in operation over one hundred years later, and in 1986 the Selection and Hanging Committee viewed 12,544 entries, of which 1,593 were eventually hung. The paintings are shown to the committee anonymously, with neither the title nor the artist revealed, and if more than one member of the committee raises their hand then the painting passes forward to the second stage of selection when they are considered again with the aim of creating 'an interesting and coherent show'.

The Royal Academy was the country's first formal art school, founded in 1768 by a group of painters who included Angelica Kauffman, Thomas Gainsborough, and Joshua Reynolds, who later became the Academy's first president; among their first students were Joseph Turner and John Constable. The Academy began life in a house in Pall Mall and moved first to Somerset House and then to Trafalgar Square, where it shared a building with the National Gallery, before finally settling at Burlington House on Piccadilly.

above
The Selection and Hanging Committee for the Royal Academy's 1987 Summer Exhibition. In 1875 an artist complained that the pictures were viewed at a rate of one every 20 seconds. May/June 1987.

opposite
Selection Committee Chairman Roger de Grey having a welcome cup of tea as he sits among some of the thousands of entries for the Royal Academy's 1987 Summer Exhibition. May/June 1987.

One of the more unusual jobs to have been undertaken by gallery workers was the unearthing of various art treasures from 'Aladdin's Cave', a deep hide-out in a disused section of the tube system below Piccadilly Circus. Paintings from the Tate Gallery and the London Museum (now amalgamated with the Museum of London) were stored there for the duration of the Second World War, and the last of them were brought to the surface in February 1946.

Some of those paintings are still on view at Tate Britain, which was built on the site of the Millbank Penitentiary as the Tate Gallery in 1897 using money donated by the sugar magnate Sir Henry Tate, who also donated his collection of 65 paintings and two sculptures. Art dealer and benfactor Sir Joseph

below
The last of hundreds of paintings to be returned to the Tate Gallery and the London Museum after war-time safe-keeping in 'Aladdin's Cave' 80 feet below Piccadilly Circus tube station. 5th February 1946.

Duveen paid for a gallery to house a bequest from Royal Academy alumnus Joseph Turner. The Turner Bequest has since been moved to the Clore Gallery, completed in 1987 with donations from the Clore Foundation and Mrs Vivien Duffield, the daughter of the late Sir Charles Clore.

Turner is widely regarded as Britain's greatest artist, and he bequeathed over one hundred paintings to the nation. He exhibited his first watercolours in the window of his father's barbershop in Covent Garden while he was still a boy, and exhibited at the Royal Academy when he was fifteen. His relatives added to his bequest, making the Turner Collection at the Tate the largest in the world with over three hundred paintings and an amazing nineteen thousand watercolours and drawings – the Tate is also the sponsor of the prestigious, and usually controversial, Turner Prize.

Sir Henry would no doubt be delighted that his name is associated with art as well as sugar, although few people make the connection. Iain Sinclair thinks of the Tate Gallery as being 'twinned with the belching treacle factory at Silvertown' and says that 'no one should be allowed to gawp at the Stanley Spencers, or lift the felt from a case of Blakes, until they have completed a tour of inspection at Silvertown, licked sugar crystals from the web of their fingers'.

The art-handlers on the escalator in 1946 cut a similar figure to London Underground workers 30 years later, carrying some slightly less valuable artwork to Charing Cross underground station. The station opened in 1870 as part of the Metropolitan District Railway, later the District Line, and changed its name on 12th September 1976 to Embankment.

The car may have killed off certain skills and trades, such as whip-minding, but it has given rise to others, among them the squeegee merchant. And the modern street-cry comes not from the vendor but from the unwilling customer – 'But I said no!' There are now well over three and a half thousand sets of traffic lights in London, and if a motorist were to be the victim of a squeegee merchant at every one it could prove very costly.

The police can alter the timing of about two-thirds of those 3,500 sets of traffic lights in response to accidents or in order to control traffic flow, giving rise to some of the myths and frustrations of driving in London – and perhaps giving the squeegee merchants an extra few seconds to ply their trade. Cab drivers talk of 'riding the green wave' on the Marylebone Road, watching the lights change ahead of them and pacing their approach with the skill of a surfer. But these are rare, magical moments, perhaps experienced on a dawn run from Heathrow. For the rest of the day drivers are more likely to be victims of the fact that a queue on the Marylebone Road won't cause a queue anywhere else, so the police who control the lights use Marylebone to 'store' excess traffic. The same is true of the southbound carriageway of Park Lane.

For a squeegee merchant with a head for heights there's always the Post Office Tower (as it was then called). He's unlikely to get people leaning out of the window with small change but the view is some compensation. This window cleaner can quite confidently claim to be London's highest, cleaning the observation windows of what was then the tallest building in Britain just before it opened to the public on 19th May 1966.

above

Squeegee 1 – a
windscreen washer
claims another victim in
Knightsbridge. c1994.

left

Squeegee 2 – a window
cleaner with altitude.
Cleaning the windows
of the observation
gallery of the Post Office
Tower shortly before it
opened to the public.
3rd May 1966.

above

Tommy Brown cleans
the sword of Justice
while workmate Alex
Hartley has a quick
cuppa in the scales.
27th August 1970.

The restaurant and observation decks may not be the highest part of the Post Office Tower, but at 520 feet the window cleaner on the previous page is considerably higher, though much safer in his cradle, than the workers precariously balanced atop the cross on the dome of St Paul's (366 feet), fixing the grasshopper on the clock tower of the Royal Exchange (177 feet) or, in true British workmanlike fashion, drinking a mug of tea in the scales of Justice at the Central Criminal Court (212 feet).

Better known as the Old Bailey, after the street on which it stands, the Central Criminal Court is distinguished by its green dome and the gilded statue of Justice holding the sword and scales. The notorious Judge Jeffreys held office at the Old Bailey and some of the country's most infamous criminal trials took place there, including those of Oscar Wilde, Dr Crippen, Lord Haw-Haw, the Kray twins, the Yorkshire Ripper, the Guildford Four and the Birmingham Six. The present court building was constructed in 1903–6 and opened by Edward VII in 1907 on the site of Newgate Gaol, which was described as 'a veritable Hell, worthy of the imagination of Dante' by one of its more famous inmates, Casanova. (Another of Casanova's comments was that: 'In London, everything is easy to him who has money and is not afraid of spending it.') Newgate Gaol also served as something of a literary academy, playing host at various times to Sir Thomas Malory, Daniel Defoe, Christopher Marlowe and Ben Jonson.

The eight-foot grasshopper on the clock tower of the Royal Exchange is a reminder of its founder, Sir Thomas Gresham. The idea of an exchange was first mooted by Gresham's father, Richard, who based his ideas on a merchant's meeting place, or Bourse, that he had seen in operation in Antwerp. His negotiations to build a Bourse in the City fell through and it was his son Thomas, ambassador to Europe and Elizabeth I's financial adviser, who eventually made his father's dream a reality. When it was completed the bell tower was topped with the symbol from the Gresham family crest – the same

above left

A family affair – three steeplejacks, brothers Jon, Fred and Ernest Walker, replace the grasshopper on top of the Royal Exchange after its removal during the war for safekeeping. The grasshopper is from the Gresham family crest and is part of the original 16th-century Royal Exchange.
12th January 1949.

above

Cleaning the cross above the dome of St Paul's Cathedral.
2nd August 1922.

grasshopper that graces the third building on the site nearly four hundred and fifty years later. There were also grasshoppers on each corner of the main building and above each dormer window. Gresham's Bourse was opened by Elizabeth I in 1570 but she disliked the word, and decreed 'that it be proclaimed the Royal Exchange, and so be called from henceforth and not otherwise', a sentiment repeated by Queen Victoria when she opened the third Royal Exchange in 1844.

The ball and cross above the dome of St Paul's are not in fact supported by the dome, which consists of a timber frame covered with Derbyshire lead, but by a brick cone built within it. The dome presented Wren with two major problems: the first was that the church authorities wanted a steeple, and he solved that problem by ignoring them; the second was that the dome as he envisaged it from the outside would be too tall for the interior proportions of the cathedral. Wren's solution was to build a smaller interior dome surmounted by the brick cone supporting the cross, with an outer dome 60 feet taller than the inner.

Although it makes less of an impact than St Paul's on the London skyline, the copper dome of the former Round Reading Room at the British Museum is one of the largest domes in the world. It was designed by Sydney Smirke as a means of extending the museum to make room for its rapidly expanding collection, and created a new interior space out of what had been a courtyard within the quadrangle of buildings previously designed by his brother Robert Smirke. At the turn of the millennium, with the removal of the British Library to new premises at St Pancras, the Reading Room was opened to the general public for the first time and history repeated itself as the Great Court was again converted into an interior space with the addition to the dome of a glass roof by Norman Foster, enclosing the whole of Robert Smirke's courtyard.

The entire edifice of the British Museum might have been at what is now Buckingham Palace, but Buckingham House was too expensive so Montagu House in Bloomsbury was chosen instead. The origins of the museum lie with Sir Hans Sloane, the wealthy Chelsea doctor after whom Sloane Square is named. During his lifetime he amassed a collection of 80,000 curios which he bequeathed to George II for £20,000. The King declined the offer, so parliament bought the collection and set up a foundation to house it, resulting in the world's first public museum. Almost immediately the museum began to make new acquisitions and receive new bequests, and before long space was inadequate. Robert Smirke rebuilt Montagu House as a quadrangle surrounding the Great Court and, only five years after it was completed, the courtyard was converted into the Round Reading Room.

Whilst not as stressful as the City trading floor, as physically taxing as carrying fish baskets, or as dangerous as scaling London's highest buildings, a great amount of edifying work was carried out under the great dome of the reading room, which played host to the likes of Charles Darwin, Samuel Beckett, Trotsky, Lenin, who worked under the pseudonym Jacob Richter, and Karl Marx, who wrote *Das Kapital* at desk 07. But perhaps the most important work connected with the museum was the invention of milk chocolate – while physician to the Governor of Jamaica, Sir Hans Sloane became the first person to mix milk with cocoa, a recipe he later sold to the Cadbury brothers.

Multi-
cultural

08

London

below
Stephen Collins,
Natasha Le Bon and
Christopher Bellot catch
a modern rickshaw
outside 'Soho institution'
Bar Italia.
2nd December 1998.

LONDON, FOUNDED BY ITALIANS, HAS always been a multi-cultural city. Little is known about the early history of the capital – there are myths that it was founded as New Troy c1240BC, and there is evidence of a Celtic settlement called Llyn-din – but the first historical evidence of a permanent settlement, and the impetus that led London to develop into a thriving city, came with the arrival of a group of Italians led by a man called Caesar. Since then London has been constantly assimilating new groups of visitors, immigrants, invaders and conquerors, from the Danish Vikings and the Norman Conquerors through the Jewish traders and Hanseatic merchants of the Middle Ages, to the Huguenot refugees and the massive wave of Commonwealth immigration since the Second World War.

But it all began with the Romans, who built bridges, roads, brothels, houses (they introduced central heating, which did not return until the 19th century) and, no doubt, the first Italian restaurants and cafés. London grew into a strong commercial centre, attracting Italian bankers to settle during the 13th century; many of them were from Lombardy, and the area where they lived and worked became known as Lombard Street. In the late 19th century a large influx of Italians created the Italian quarter in Clerkenwell and Holborn that is still known as Little Italy and although the Italian community has now dispersed across London Little Italy, with St Peter's Italian Church at its centre, is still a focus for London's 75,000-plus Italians (the 1991 census recorded 30,052 of them as being Italian-born).

Many of the 19th-century immigrants worked in the catering trade, and today London's numerous Italian restaurants, coffee bars and delicatessens remain extremely popular, particularly those in Soho. *Bar Italia* opened in 1949, a tiny stand-up café whose clientèle spills out onto Frith Street at all times of the day and night. Open almost around-the-clock, it is very popular with those wanting to watch Italian-league soccer on the giant video screen at the back of the café.

Soho was split in two by the building of Shaftesbury Avenue and after the war the area to the south developed into Chinatown. Peter and Mario's Italian trattoria, founded by Peter Rizzi in 1933, was the last non-Chinese restaurant on Gerrard Street, looking somewhat incongruous beneath the Chinese lettering of the road sign. It closed its doors for the last time in December 1986 after more than 50 years' trading. The restaurant was a family business run by two couples, Fred and Tina Rizzi and Romano and Gloria Conti; Fred Rizzi and Gloria Conti (née Rizzi) were brother and sister, children of the restaurant's founder, who married another brother and sister, Romano and Tina Conti (now Rizzi).

below

Peter Mario, the last
non-Chinese restaurant
on Gerrard Street, seen
the day after it closed its
doors for the last time
having been in business
for 50 years.
4th December 1986.

below left
Chinese market stalls on
Gerrard Street.
(Not dated.)

below
Pagoda-style telephone
kiosks with Chinese
lettering add to the
atmosphere of
Chinatown.
September 1991.

below left
Chinese market stalls on
Gerrard Street.
(Not dated.)

Gerrard Street is the main street of Chinatown,
one of London's most distinctive ethnic areas,
although few of the city's 60,000 Chinese actually
live in this small part of Soho. The first Chinese
immigrants arrived in the late 18th and early 19th
century on the ships of the East India Company
and settled near the docks around Limehouse,
which became London's first Chinatown; by the
First World War there were more than thirty
Chinese shops and restaurants in Limehouse
Causeway and Pennyfields. Wartime bomb
damage and postwar demolition led to the
decline of Limehouse Chinatown but in the
meantime a new influx of immigrants began to
arrive from the New Territories and Hong Kong,
and started to buy up the then cheap and run-

below
Pagoda-style telephone
kiosks with Chinese
lettering add to the
atmosphere of
Chinatown.
September 1991.

down property in Gerrard Street, leading to the development of a new Chinatown between Shaftesbury Avenue and Leicester Square.

Most of the immigrants arriving in the 1950s and '60s were employed in the catering industry, answering a new demand for Chinese food said to have been sparked off by the fact that British soldiers had acquired a taste for oriental cuisine while posted abroad. Others followed the 'pioneers' who had set up shops and restaurants on Gerrard Street, and by the 1970s the area had become the focus for the Chinese community, known to them as *Tong Yan Kai*, or Chinese Street. And Chinatown is not just about Chinese restaurants; there are also Chinese supermarkets, Chinese market stalls, and shops selling Chinese arts and crafts, ceramics, games, herbal medicines, books and imported newspapers, all of which creates a unique atmosphere that has been reinforced with pagoda-style telephone kiosks, oriental archways and street signs in English and Chinese.

Chinatown is a huge tourist attraction, especially at Chinese New Year, which has been celebrated here since 1973 with the colourful Chinese lion dances. In China the celebrations are spread out over several weeks but in Britain they are concentrated on the Sunday closest to the Chinese New Year's Day, which is governed by the lunar calendar and usually falls in late January or early February. But, more importantly than being a tourist attraction, Chinatown is first and foremost a working part of the Chinese community, and still plays an important rôle in the life of Chinese ex-pats, who come to Chinatown for special occasions such as wedding receptions and birthdays, or simply to eat and shop amongst other Chinese.

London's ethnic diversification since the Second World War is now starting to be reflected in the fabric of the city; not just in the oriental archways and telephone boxes of Chinatown and the bilingual street signs of Chinatown and Whitechapel, but also in the appearance of landmark buildings such as the London Central Mosque close to Regent's Park and the East London Mosque on Whitechapel Road, whose minarets and copper domes make a striking addition to the London skyline.

The London Central Mosque, first mooted in the 1920s, was completed in 1978, its oriental architecture a suitable addition to a park laid out for the Prince Regent, whose most celebrated architectural project was the Brighton Pavilion. The mosque was designed by Frederick Gibberd & Partners (Gibberd was also the architect of the adventurous Liverpool Roman Catholic Cathedral) and built from 1972–78. Egyptian-born Mohamed El Sharkawy, who has spent the last 10 years as an Imam at the mosque and has brought up his family in London, invites 'all peoples of all religions to enter as a visitor, a student of Arabic culture or a seeker after truth'.

The East London Mosque was built to serve the Muslims of the East End's growing Bengali community, and opened in July 1985 on Whitechapel Road with the help of a £1 million donation from the Saudi-Arabian government. Whitechapel and Spitalfields have seen many of London's immigrant populations arrive and disperse before receiving fresh waves of newcomers. In the 1650s Sephardic Jews from Portugal and Spain settled here, followed at the end of the century by French Huguenots (who brought with them the word 'refugee'), then Irish Catholics who, ironically, built most of the area's Protestant churches. The late 19th century saw a huge influx of Ashkenazi Jews escaping the Russian and Polish pogroms and most recently, since the 1960s, the area has been host to the Bengalis, who now work in the garment trade pioneered in the area by the Huguenots and continued by the Ashkenazim. And like the Huguenots and Jews before them, who built churches and synagogues respectively, the Bengalis have added their place of worship to the architectural heritage of the East End.

below right
The London Central
Mosque at Regent's
Park.
7th July 1977.

right
The East London Mosque
in Whitechapel nearing
completion.
13th April 1985.

Just north of Whitechapel Road, running through Spitalfields, is Brick Lane, scene of one of London's most celebrated Sunday markets and now the centre of the Bengali community, where 'each step is accompanied by the smell of spices from the numerous cafés and restaurants, the bright colours of the fabrics which line the clothes-shop windows, and the heavy beat of bhangra music from music shops and passing cars'. Halal butchers, saree centres, Indian sweetmarts and newsagents selling Bengali papers all add to the Asian atmosphere, as do the orthodox Muslim men who always wear their distinctive white skull caps or oval fur hats.

And yet only a century ago Brick Lane was at the heart of what Jewish novelist Israel Zangwill called 'a stronghold of hard-sell Judaism… into which no missionary dared set foot'. The way in which the legacy of successive waves of immigrants has been assimilated and adapted by the next is exemplified by one building, now a mosque, on the corner of Fournier Street and Brick Lane. Fournier Street was originally called Church Street, an early Georgian terrace with especially long windows in the roofs, designed to allow light into the weaver's attics first used by the Huguenots. In 1743 the Huguenots established a church on the corner which became the Spitalfields Great Synagogue in 1897 and has been used as the *Jamme Masjid*, or Great Mosque, since 1975.

Another sign of cultural change, in addition to the transformation of butchers from charcuterie to kosher to halal, and buildings from church to synagogue to mosque, are the posters for Bengali Super Stars playing at the Wembley Arena.

above
Orthodox Muslims on the corner of Brick Lane and Princelet Street.
18th September 1993.

right
Brick Lane's bilingual street sign.
18th September 1993.

above

Shoppers at the Brick
Lane market pass
posters for the Bengali
Super Stars at the
Wembley Arena.
26th March 1996.

right
Thousands of Hindus
march from Hyde Park to
Trafalgar Square to
celebrate the opening of
the Shree Swaminarayan
Mandir, a Hindu temple
in Neasden.
18th August 1995.

below right
Mrs Upadhaya, Mrs
Padhak (with the milk
bottle), Mrs Bance and
Mrs Dhir wait to feed
offerings of milk to an
image of The Shivji
inside the Vishwa
Temple in Southall.
22nd September 1995.

above
Hindu monks immersing an image of a deity in the waters of the Thames at Petersham Meadows as part of the ceremony of Jal Zilani. 29th September 1974.

As well as synagogues and mosques, *mandir*, or Hindu temples, are becoming part of the landscape of the capital. The Shree Swaminarayan Mandir in Neasden appears in *The Guinness Book of Records* as the largest Hindu temple outside Asia, with a prayer hall capable of holding more than four thousand worshippers. The temple was consecrated in August 1995, when thousands of Hindus marched from Hyde Park to Trafalgar Square in celebration; the Hindu women seen here are carrying *khalash*, a sacred ceremonial coconut that contains the pure water of life. Sadhu Atmaswarupdas, head of the *mandir*, welcomes all people to visit the temple whatever their country, race, religion or colour. Born in Tanzania, he says, 'I enjoy cosmopolitan London, I like the way people are so interested in other customs, cultures and traditions. In this multiracial city this temple acts as a seat of understanding and encourages a harmonious way of living together.'

As with the Chinese, the first Indians to come to London were sailors who arrived in the 18th century on the ships of the East India Company, some of whom settled in the area around The Highway in the East End. But this was a transient population, and it was not until the 1920s and 1930s that a stable Indian community was established. After the Second World War thousands of Indian and Pakistani immigrants came to London, many of them settling in Southall, now home of the Vishwa Temple where worshippers are seen here waiting to take part in a ceremony feeding gifts of milk to a statue of The Shivji. (The commonest form of worship for Hindus is a *puja*, which involves presenting offerings to a *murti*, or image of a deity.)

The first Hindus called themselves Aryans – the name Hindu was originally used by Muslim invaders in the 8th century as a derivation of 'Sindhu', the name of the River Indus, where scenes like the one above on the banks of the Thames at Petersham Meadows must have been quite common. Here Hindu monks are immersing a *murti* in the river as part of the ceremony of Jal Zilani.

above
Orthodox Jews
protesting outside the
Israeli Tourist Board in
Great Marlborough
Street.
5th December 1995.

The longest-established of London's immigrant cultures is Judaism. The Romans left in the 5th century and the Danes were kicked out by Alfred the Great but the Jews, first invited to England by William the Conqueror, came to stay – albeit with a hiatus of 366 years between being expelled by Edward I and readmitted by Cromwell. The Crown's relationship with the Jewish community was always one of convenience rather than respect, giving them the status of resident aliens with no legal rights, so that they were dependent entirely on royal favour for their protection. Jewish financiers set up in what was known as Jew's Street, later Old Jewry, and successive monarchs raised money from them by taking a large share of the profits from their money-lending, which was regulated by the Crown. During the reign of Henry II the Jews provided about a twelfth of the royal income but their success was to be their downfall, because by the middle of the 13th century their wealth and power were thought to be a threat to the Crown. Edward I imprisoned all the Jews in the kingdom, ransomed them for £20,000, and in 1290 expelled them from the country.

Three and a half centuries later it was anti-Semitism in mainland Europe that brought the Jews back to England, many Sephardim arriving from Spain and Portugal from 1540 onwards to escape the Inquisition. Judaism was still illegal in England and until 1656, when Cromwell granted Jews the right to worship in their homes, they had to pretend to be Christians. From the 17th century onwards Jews arrived from all over Europe to escape persecution and pogroms, settling mainly in the East End and

below
Jewish schoolchildren
with one of their
teachers as they wait to
go off to Chessington
Zoo to celebrate Lag
Bo'omer. 9th May 1993.

bottom
The fifth Beatle?
A member of the
Orthodox Jewish
community on a
zebra crossing in
Golder's Green.
1st October 1992.

often working in tailors' sweatshops: by 1901 over forty-five per cent of London's Jews worked in the clothing industry. As the East End Jews flourished they left the East End to the next wave of immigrants and moved out to the suburbs, particularly to the north. Their movement can be traced by the establishment of synagogues in Dalston (1885), Stoke Newington (1903), Finsbury Park (1912), Stamford Hill (1915) and Golders Green (1922).

In December 1995 Orthodox Jews protested outside the Israeli Tourist Board in Great Marlborough Street against the desecration of 1st century Macabean graves found during the building of a new road in Israel and, on a happier occasion in January 2000, Jewish schoolchildren gathered in central London under the stern gaze of their teacher for a trip to Chessington Zoo to celebrate the holiday of Lag Bo'omer, the Jewish day of peace and unity.

left
Passing on the skills –
the African beat in
Balham. 9th August
1974.

below
Watched by a crowd of inquisitive children, John Prince tests the ivories in his London workshop. 6th September 1961.

bottom
A service at Westminster Abbey celebrating Britain's links with the Caribbean. 27th April 1986.

On 27th April 1986 people of Caribbean descent held religious services all over the country to celebrate the Caribbean and its links with Britain. The photograph below shows the priest and some of those providing music for the main service at Westminster Abbey, including the Jamaican Folk Singers and members of the Trinidadian Casablanca Steel Orchestra.

Britain's links with the Caribbean began in the 17th century; the first English settlement was established on St Kitts in 1623, soon followed by setlements on Barbados, Antigua and Montserrat, and in 1655 a Cromwellian expedition took Jamaica from the Spanish. Like the Spanish before them, the British established sugar plantations and transported black slaves from Africa to labour on them. Britain's slave trade became the worst in the world, carrying over forty per cent of all slaves transported between 1701 and 1800; 348,000 people were sent to North America, and nearly 1.5 million forced to work on the sugar plantations of the Caribbean. Although some West Africans had come to Britain after the opening up of trade links in the 16th century the first significant influx of black people to Britain was during the 17th and 18th centuries, when plantation owners and colonial administrators who were returning home brought their slaves with them. The free black population, mainly West African seamen and slaves who had bought their freedom, settled near the docks in Limehouse and Ratcliff, and later in Canning Town.

As a result the black population of Georgian London rose as high as 10,000 but, as with the Chinese and Asian communities, the modern wave of immigration is unconnected with these early immigrants, who arrived as sailors working the trade routes (and in this case as slaves); the later arrivals came as a result of new opportunities arising after the Second World War. West Indians and West Africans arrived during the war to serve in the armed forces or work in munitions factories, and after the war many more were recruited directly from the Caribbean and Africa by the National Health Service, British Rail and London Transport. Immigration from the Caribbean slowed down after the 1960s while there was an increase in the number of people arriving from Africa, who now make up nearly a third of London's black population.

Of the West Indian immigrants arriving immediately after the Second World War, most of the Jamaicans settled in Brixton, giving the area the strong Afro-Caribbean consciousness that it retains today. Like most of south London's Victorian suburbs, Brixton's transformation from open fields to a scattering of large houses owned by rich City merchants came with the opening of new bridges across the Thames (in this case Vauxhall Bridge, in 1816); with the coming of the railways this development then quickly accelerated into much denser, less affluent housing. The house-building boom sparked by the railways and, later, by the extension of tram and horse-bus services from Westminster, led to an article in the *Builder* asking 'how so many private residences can find occupants', a question that seemed unthinkable a century later when many of the large private houses had been sub-divided into lodging-houses.

Cheap lodgings, and easy access to the West End, meant that Brixton became a favourite with those working in the theatre: music hall stars Dan Leno and Fred Karno lived in Brixton and, more recently, former Prime Minister John Major spent part of his childhood there – his father, a music hall and circus performer, had lodgings on Coldharbour Lane. Cheap lodgings also attracted the first wave of post-war immigrants from the Caribbean, who arrived from Jamaica in 1948 on the liner *Empire Windrush* and settled in the streets around Somerleyton Road, Akerman Road and later Railton Road. Although Brixton is often thought of as a black ghetto, an idea reinforced by the riots there in 1981 and 1985, its thriving market, Ritzy cinema and trendy bars and clubs all give it a far more positive image than 15-year-old news reports.

opposite top
The Notting Hill Carnival
passes *The Eagle*.
27th August 2000.

opposite bottom
Notting Hill Carnival.
27th August 2000.

While most of the Jamaicans arriving from the Caribbean after the war settled in Brixton, Trinidadians came to Notting Hill. In 1958 the homes of the West Indian immigrants were attacked by busloads of whites protesting against mass immigration, and the Notting Hill carnival was set up unofficially the following year to promote racial harmony. At that time the carnival was little more than a street party; simply a few church hall events and a carnival parade inspired by the Trinidadian Ash Wednesday carnivals that the new arrivals had grown up with. In 1965 the carnival was officially established as a local pageant and fair, by 1985 it had become London's most popular public event, and it has since grown into the world's biggest street festival outside Rio, with over a million people now estimated to take to the streets of Notting Hill for the three-day extravaganza on August Bank Holiday weekend.

The highlights of the carnival are the costume parades on Sunday and Monday, which make their way round a three-mile circuit taking in Ladbroke Grove, Westbourne Grove, Chepstow Road, Great Western Road and Kensal Road. The procession is made up of trucks carrying the sound systems and *mas* (masquerade) bands, followed on foot by the costumed masqueraders and dancers. Those not actually taking part in the parades can soak up the sound of the steel bands (and the reggae, ragga, jungle and hip-hop), borrow policemen's helmets or simply pig out on Red Stripe and curried goat.

London – the

09

Bleaker Side

below

A former Victorian
workhouse, Peckham.
13th October 1990.

LIKE ALL MAJOR CITIES, LONDON has its bleaker side, caused by a combination of poverty, decay, overcrowding, bad urban planning, and anti-social behaviour. The starting point for many other ills is bad housing. Often the finger is pointed at high-rise tower blocks but in most cases the Victorian slum terraces they replaced were even worse. Nineteenth-century illustrations by the French artist Gustav Doré provide a visual record of the desolate housing conditions in the London described by Charles Dickens: rows of terraced houses under a pall of smoke, crammed back-to-back in the shadow of the railway arches. Slum clearances did not help, improving the housing in a given area but at such a cost that the previous occupants could no longer afford to live there and were simply driven out to other already crowded slums. Ninety years later the smoke may have cleared but otherwise the back yard of

this terraced house in Camberwell looks much the same as Doré's 1871 illustration, although fortunately sights like this were much rarer by 1960.

In 1855 an article in *Builder* claimed that 'the wretched lodgings of the poor are the cause of more than half the misery now existing'. The *Builder* was referring to slum terraces and 'rookeries', former middle-class houses that had been turned into tenements, but the sentiment is often heard today with reference to tower blocks and housing estates. Between the wars a number of 'model estates' were built that radically improved London's housing situation and 'contributed to the disappearance of the bare-foot urchin'. At that time tower blocks were rejected as 'quite unsuitable for a working-class population… [the] self-contained house is what appeals to working people', but unfortunately the advice was later ignored. Post-war developments built upwards and soon became the new slums.

During the 19th century the population of London rose from just over one million in 1801 (the first official census) to nearly seven million a hundred years later. The growing number of destitute people on the streets led to the Poor Law Amendment Act of 1834, which formalized workhouses (initially an Elizabethan idea), tried unsuccessfully to ensure that there would be no poor relief outside the workhouse, and stigmatized poor relief to such a degree that instead of being a basic right it became a source of shame. In a reversal of the Elizabethan ideal, where workhouses provided 'a disciplined and productive environment for the able-bodied poor', Victorian workhouses became notorious as 'prison hospitals for the penniless', and were known as 'bastilles' to many of their potential inmates, who would no doubt be delighted to see the demise of this former workhouse in Peckham (opposite).

Many social ills can be blamed on poverty
and bad housing but football hooliganism is
not one of them. Hooliganism is a much older
phenomenon than the term used to describe it
(the word only came into use at the end of the
19th century) and it is not a problem exclusive
to London, although the term 'hooligan' is in fact
the name of an Irish family who lived in south-
east London and allegedly went around
destroying property for no apparent reason.
Ernest Weekly, in his *Romance of Words*, adds
a touch of romance to an irredeemably ugly form
of behaviour: 'The original Hooligans were a
spirited Irish family of that name whose
proceedings enlivened the drab monotony of life
in Southwark towards the end of the 19th
century.'

Some social historians claim that
hooliganism is a form of behaviour which
attached itself to football having come from
'youth cults' in other areas of life – if so then it
is perhaps an example of things coming full
circle, because in April 1590 three journeymen
were imprisoned for 'outrageously and riotously
behaving themselves at football play in
Cheapside'. Two years later the Duke of
Württemburg complained that London
apprentices 'care little for foreigners but scoff
and laugh at them; and moreover one dare not
oppose them, else the street-boys and
apprentices collect together in immense crowds
and strike to the right and left unmercifully
without any regard to person', and Pepys
records gangs of youths, variously referred to as
Hectors, Scourers and Mohawks, who roamed
the streets of London 'leering at young ladies
and pushing old gentlemen'.

During the 20th century media attention, and
therefore public concern, centred on the Teddy

Boys in the 1950s and the pitched seaside battles of the Mods and Rockers in the 1960s. By the 1970s
gang violence had attached itself to football, where it has remained for 30 years despite social
research into the causes, the introduction and removal of cages to segregate rival fans, and
international police efforts against known ringleaders. The introduction of all-seater stadiums in 1994
eased the problem slightly but violence outside the grounds and confrontations with the police, such
as those shown here in 1971 and 1999, are still a common occurrence.

below left
A homeless man looks
for his Christmas
breakfast in a litter bin.
25th December 1992.

below
Sam raises a toast in
Hackney.
3rd February 1994.

While lager leads to loutish behaviour among those rich enough to buy designer beer in bottles like the Arsenal fan on the previous page, it only causes sadness and decrepitude among those for whom the high point of the day is a swig of super-strength from a can — the average life expectancy for rough sleepers, many of whom are also street drinkers, is a mere 42 years.

Drinking is nothing new to the streets of London; in the 18th century the chosen drink of the poor was gin because it was so cheap — 'drunk for a penny, dead drunk for tuppence' — and by the 1740s London's consumption of gin averaged two pints a week for every man, woman and child in the city. During the 18th century novelist, lawyer and J.P. Henry Fielding, co-founder of the Bow Street Runners, wrote that gin was 'the principal sustenance (if it may be called so) of more than a hundred thousand people in the metropolis', and 250 years later

alcohol is still the principal sustenance of many of London's poorest: one of these homeless men searches for his breakfast in a litter bin (on Christmas Day, 1992) but the other two find it at the bottom of a can.

Fielding's observations were reinforced by Hogarth's famous prints comparing the pleasures of Beer Street with the miseries of Gin Lane (although in these 20th-century photographs Beer Street looks just as miserable), and in 1751 the Gin Act was passed with the intention of curbing 'immoderate drinking of distilled spiritous liquor by persons of the meanest and lowest sort'. However, in the end, it was the increasing price of gin that placed gin beyond the means of the poor, and led to its adoption as a polite middle-class apéritif. Street-drinkers turned to cheap wine, giving rise to the term 'wino', and then to cider and high-strength lager.

And drinking is not just the result of boredom or low self-esteem: figures collated by the charity Crisis show that 45 per cent of beggars and street drinkers have a dependency problem, which in itself is part of a much bigger problem – the same figures indicate that more than 40 per cent of beggars started begging to get money for drink or drugs, and that for one third of rough sleepers alcohol was a contributory factor to their first episode of sleeping rough.

Sleeping outside every night on the streets of London is the norm for more than four hundred people, half of the total for the rest of the country put together, and an estimated five times that number will sleep rough on at least one night during the course of a year. Homelessness is nothing new but it is on the increase: between 1979 and 1990 the number of homeless people in London increased tenfold, from 8,000 to 80,000 (including those sleeping rough, those in hostels, B&Bs and squats, and the 'hidden homeless'). During the same period waiting lists for council housing rose to around 400,000 while council building programmes were reduced from 9,131 new starts in 1979 to a pitiful 302 in 1990. Social historian Roy Porter summarises the homeless situation in 1990s London:

> Homelessness – eradicated by the mid twentieth century – became endemic again during the Thatcher years. Swarms of dossers and vagrants reappeared, cardboard cities sprouting in the luxuriance of yuppie affluence. An encampment of tramps and the homeless arose at the Waterloo Bridge roundabout, fifty yards from the Festival of Britain site and next to the National Theatre, while elegant Lincoln's Inn Fields became a Third World shanty town for scores of the homeless – a settlement tolerated for several years, since no-one wished to assume responsibility. As in Third World countries, thousands in London now beg by day ('homeless and hungry') and sleep rough in shop doorways and church porches…

Porter could add bridges, telephone boxes and shopping centre rubbish tips to his list of sleeping-places. These photographs were taken one in each of the last three decades of the 20th century, and the picture becomes more and more bleak: in 1971, a tramp hanging out his washing on Blackfriars Bridge, in 1984, Leo waking up to start the day in his telephone box home, and in 1990 a man lying in the Brunswick Centre, discarded by society like the rubbish amongst which he sleeps, in a part of London described by Isabella in Jane Austen's *Emma*: 'Our part of London is so very superior to most others… We are so very airy.'

Leo, who lived in a phone box in Wandsworth, was discovered not by a survey into London's homeless, nor in an attempt to find him proper accommodation, but by a newspaper survey into telephone boxes following a survey by *Which?* magazine into the telephone service. The original caption for this photograph says that 'despite complaints from local residents… Leo continues to sleep in the box each night'. And BT's solution to the 'problem'? They disconnected the phone.

below
Leo, who slept every night in this telephone box in Wandsworth. 2nd February 1984.

above

A tramp hangs out his
washing on Blackfriars
Bridge. 16th June 1971.

right

Homelessness in the
Brunswick Centre, a
'very superior' part of
London. 29th July 1990.

But there is hope amidst the squalor and, despite the complaints and the grumbling from local residents who do not like to see poverty on their doorstep, there are charitable souls left among the population of London: in the run-up to Christmas 1984 the charity Crisis at Christmas received donations of 1,600 suits, 5,000 shirts, 200 hats and 650 mattresses to help London's homeless through the festive season.

Crisis at Christmas has since changed its name to Crisis and has become a national charity whose mission statement is 'to end street homelessness through practical action to help homeless people move towards a secure, sustainable home'. Crisis was founded in 1967 in response to the television documentary *Cathy Come Home*, after which more than 3,000 people gathered for a candlelit vigil in Hyde Park to demonstrate their support for homeless people – an event which is still commemorated in an annual 'pilgrimage' from Canterbury to London.

In 1972 Crisis opened its first Christmas shelter for street homeless people, a concept which is still a major element of the charity's winter services, giving homeless and vulnerably housed people an opportunity to celebrate Christmas in comfort and safety. In a project called 'London Open Christmas', Crisis now runs five Christmas shelters in the capital between 23 and 30 December, offering help, advice and companionship at a time of year which can be particularly lonely for those without a home or family. The project also offers services such as housing benefits advice, medical, eye and dental care, chiropody, counselling, and hairdressing in addition to accommodation and healthy food.

As well as the Christmas shelters that have become its trademark, Crisis has developed other schemes which now help over 20,000 homeless people a year throughout the country, including ReachOut, a network of specialist workers helping long term rough sleepers access the services they need, SmartMove, a deposit guarantee scheme enabling homeless people to buy their own homes,

and FareShare, a scheme which redistributes surplus food from supermarkets and sandwich bars to day centres and night shelters for homeless people. And Crisis is also sending out a message of hope, giving credence to government proposals that have been dismissed as hot air by the media: 'These are exciting times for Crisis and for homeless people. In December 1999, the government announced its strategy for reducing the number of people sleeping rough by two-thirds by 2002. We believe that the time has now come to end mass street homelessness for good.'

right
Prostitutes' cards in a
London phone box.
25th March 1999.

Ninety per cent of rough sleepers are men and, according to the charity Crisis, 'the low profile of women in homelessness statistics can probably be accounted for by the fact that women… make better use of their social networks than [men] to find alternative solutions to their housing problems'. It is also because a lot of homeless women are forced into prostitution.

The country's first brothel appeared in Southwark and was used by the Roman soldiers guarding London Bridge, although prostitution itself has been around a lot longer than that. The Roman brothels developed into the 'Bankside stews' that became part of the Bishop of Winchester's estate in the early 12th century, and until the 16th century successive bishops supplemented their revenue through fines and rents from the brothels, giving rise to the nickname Winchester Geese for the Bankside prostitutes. During the 17th century prostitution moved to Covent Garden, one of the first brothels in the area being the *Rose Tavern* on Russell Street, where Pepys writes of 'frigging with Doll Lane' in his 1667 *Diary*. By the early 18th century the piazza was known as 'the great square of Venus', where whores stood in the windows of the brothels and 'in a most impudent manner invited passengers from the theatres into the houses'.

Next it was Soho's turn: in the 19th century the area was described as 'a reeking home of filthy vice' and by the Second World War prostitution in Soho was big business, run by organized gangs with the connivance of the police: in 1976 ten Scotland Yard officers were jailed for bribery and corruption. Sex-shops, peep-shows and cards in telephone boxes still abound in Soho but the combined efforts of the Soho Society and Westminster Council successfully reduced the number of premises being used by the sex industry from 185 in 1982 to about 30 in 1992.

But the Soho Society and Westminster Council did not succeed in stopping vulnerable or homeless women and girls from having to take to the streets; they simply moved prostitution on elsewhere, and at the start of the 21st century one of London's most notorious areas for drug-pushing and prostitution is King's Cross. During the 1860s Hipppolyte Twain wrote about prostitutes lining the Haymarket and the Strand, but his words could be just as true of King's Cross today: 'This is not debauchery which flaunts itself but destitution – and such destitution… That is a plague-spot – the real plague-spot of English society.'

Despite the harsh reality of women standing on street corners in King's Cross, Soho still has a reputation as London's centre for sex because of the up-front way in which the revue bars, clubs, peep shows, magazine and video shops unashamedly advertise their presence in neon. But the sex industry in Soho is now only a fraction of what it was during the 1960s and '70s when it reached its peak as a highly lucrative business both for the gangs involved in organizing it and for those members of the police force who were later convicted of running a massive protection racket.

One of the earliest gangs to move in on the Soho vice racket was run by the Messina Brothers, who came to London from Malta, and it was later taken over by their former henchman Bernie Silver, Soho's 'Godfather', who was sent down in 1974. High-profile 'celebrity' gangsters such as the Messina Brothers, John McVicar, the Great Train Robbers and the Kray Twins seem to have gone out of fashion: modern gang-based crime is a lower-profile, anonymous business, and usually drugs-related. The Kray funerals in 1995 and 2000 marked the end of an era that had already passed into folklore, romanticised by pop-stars playing criminals in films such as *McVicar*, *Buster*, and *The Krays*.

'There's been nothing to touch it since Churchill,' said the florist who provided the floral tributes for Ronnie Kray's hearse; and she was right, not just about the volume of flowers but also the six black-plumed horses and the crowds, the cameras and the television crews that lined the streets. This was the East End's State Funeral, the era of 1960s' gangland resurrected for a few short hours on 29th March 1995 for the send-off of Ronnie Kray, aka 'the Colonel'.

If the Krays had not already been mythical figures then the pomp and circumstance of this funeral, the 26 stretch limousines, the minders, the helicopters, the media attention and the police presence would have made them so: it is said that those not in the know asked whether the Queen Mother had died.

The Kray twins carved out their place in London legend through a combination of persona, violence, demonisation by the press, and a Robin Hood image born of charitable donations and good deeds within the local community. (East End actor Billy Murray, who plays DS Beech in the television programme *The Bill*, tells how his grant for drama school was late and he faced missing the course until the Krays lent him the money.)

Ronnie's lavish, no-expense-spared funeral, with the black-plumed horses and the press enclosures dotted along the crowd-lined route from English's funeral parlour to St Matthew's Church, did nothing to diminish the mythical status of the Kray twins, and five years later it was Reggie's turn, with a smaller turn-out but still with the shaven-headed minders and the traditional six black horses pulling the hearse.

In August 1958 Pembridge Road in Notting Hill became the focus of the country's first race riots, precipitated by a massive increase in Commonwealth immigration as people tried to enter the country before strict new immigration controls came into force in 1961. Busloads of whites attacked West Indian homes in the area, smashing windows and throwing petrol bombs; those riots, at least, had a positive outcome, with the Notting Hill Carnival starting unofficially the following year to promote racial harmony.

Elsewhere racial tensions simmered, and erupted again during the 1980s with riots in Brixton and on the Broadwater Farm estate in Tottenham. But this time the reasons were different. In the 1950s the established population had reacted violently to an influx of outsiders but in the 1980s the riots were precipitated by discontent among the so-called immigrant population, many of whom were now second-generation Londoners: where the Notting Hill riots were about whites responding to a perceived threat, the Brixton and Tottenham riots were about black and white members of the community expressing their feelings of resentment and social exclusion. These were not so much race riots as demonstrations against poverty, unemployment, bad housing and insensitive policing.

above
A convenience store wrecked during rioting on the Broadwater Farm estate. October 1985.

right
Looking through a smashed shopfront window at the aftermath of the Brixton riots. 12th April 1981.

above
Railton Road, Brixton,
two weeks after the
riots. 17th April 1981.

In April 1981 hundreds of youths fought with the police in the streets of Brixton, which was described as 'a major centre of London's black population' although in fact blacks and Asians made up only 29 per cent of the population and those fighting included both black and white. The violence erupted as a result of 'Operation Swamp 81', a crackdown on street crime that swamped an already tense area with police – when one youth was arrested in Wiltshire Road the crowd tried to free him and the confrontation escalated into a full-scale riot. Afterwards Metropolitan Police Commissioner Sir David McNee said that police–community relations had been as good as could be expected but the level of crime in Brixton demanded 'a strong police presence'. Riots broke out again in September 1985 when Cherry Groce was shot during a police raid (the policeman concerned was cleared of criminal charges in January 1987) and just nine days later the Broadwater Farm riot was sparked off by the death of a woman during a police search of her flat.

Broadwater Farm won prizes for its planning when it was built in 1970 but 'declined into a housing hell and a nursery of crime'. A report commissioned by the Archbishop of Canterbury and published the year after the riots could have been referring specifically to the estate when it criticized 'the architect-designed system-built slums of our post-war era', talked of 'poor design, defects in construction, poor upkeep', and noted that 'the degeneration of many such areas has now gone so far that they are in effect "separate territories" outside the mainstream of our social and economic life'.

To many people the only surprise was that the violence had not erupted sooner.

above

Offices near South
Quay on the Isle of Dogs,
destroyed by an IRA
bomb.
11th February 1996.

The objective of the Irish Republican Army is implicit in its title: the union of Northern Ireland with the Republic of Ireland. After the Anglo-Irish war of 1919–21 and a guerrilla war against the new Irish Free State from 1921–23, the IRA remained undecided as to how best to achieve its stated objective: whether to wage a campaign against the border, or to continue to fight the government, or to act politically, focussing on social and economic issues. After an ineffective border campaign from 1956–61 the IRA exerted most of its influence as a Marxist pressure group, but after the outbreak of violence in Derry and Belfast from 1969 the organisation split into the nationalist Provisional IRA and the Marxist Official IRA. The Provisional IRA then began a high-profile terrorist campaign which was instrumental in bringing about the collapse of the Stormont government in 1972, although this took it no closer to its objective, with direct rule being imposed from Westminster.

To begin with the Provisional IRA perpetrated most of its acts of terrorism in Northern Ireland but, after the ceasefire of 1974–75, began concentrating its activities on London. The campaign of terror was partially effective on a practical level, causing widespread damage and disruption, but it was never politically useful, reaping opprobrium against the means rather than winning support for the

cause. (The IRA even lost some support from the US when it was incorrectly linked with a terrorist bombing on US soil at the Atlanta Olympics.)

The IRA announced a ceasefire in August 1994 which ended on 10th February 1996 with the bombing of office buildings at South Quay, close to Canary Wharf on the Isle of Dogs. The bombing resulted in roadblocks being set up at random around the City by mobile armed police units to supplement the 'ring of steel', a series of checkpoints which had been in place throughout the ceasefire monitoring all vehicles passing in and out of the Square Mile.

London

Oddities

above
Schoolboys stop to read
the plaque marking the
centre of London.
23rd April 1955.

opposite
Three schoolchildren
stare up at Louise
Bourgeouis' enormous
spider in the Turbine Hall
at the Tate Modern.
5th May 2000.

LONDON ODDITIES IS A COLLECTION of photographs showing the quirky, hidden or unusual side of life in the capital, starting with the absolute centre of London. On 23rd April 1955 newspapers reported that it had finally been decided where the centre of London lay, and that a plaque had been laid in the pavement of Whitehall to mark the spot. These schoolboys have stopped to read the inscription, while 45 years later children at the first Annual Artworks Awards invert the boys' stooped pose, craning their necks to view Louise Bourgeouis' enormous spider in the Turbine Hall of the former Bankside Power Station, now the Tate Modern.

The site of the plaque indicating the centre of London was first marked by Edward I in the 13th century when he erected the Queen Eleanor's Cross at Charing, later known simply as the Charing Cross. Charing was a small hamlet whose name is thought to derive from the Old English word *cierran*, meaning turn; the road from Bath turned here to follow the curve of the river. After Edward I's queen, Eleanor of Castille, died in Nottinghamshire in 1290, the King erected 12 crosses at the places where her funeral cortège rested on its way to Westminster Abbey; the Charing Cross was the last of the 12, and stood where the equestrian statue of Charles I stands now on the south side of Traflagar Square.

Twentieth-century bureaucrats may have belatedly designated this the centre and marked it with a plaque but Charing Cross has long been considered the centre of the capital, metaphorically if not literally. In the 17th century it was said that anyone who wanted to know what was going on in London 'had merely to go to Charing Cross to be told'; Dr Johnson, in reply to a comment by Boswell about Fleet Street, said 'Why, sir, Fleet Street has a very animated appearance; but I think the full tide of human existence is at Charing Cross', and Dickens the younger points out that 'Charing Cross is a position rather than a place… It is the titular centre of London and the point from which all distances are measured. A line drawn N and S through it may be said to separate the London of pleasure and fashion from that of work and business'.

below left

A schoolboy checks his
watch against the clock
on the wall of the Royal
Observatory at
Greenwich.
23rd February 1968.

The centre of the world is just west of the centre of London at Greenwich, where one young schoolboy checks his watch against the definitive Greenwich Mean Time (he could also check exactly how tall he is because set into the Observatory wall next to him are the standard measures for the yard and the foot). But just as the centre of London is an arbitrary point rather than a given one, so is the Prime Meridian, and Greenwich has officially been the centre of the world only since 1884 when it was agreed at the International Meridian Conference in Washington, DC; before that date each country often used the longitude of its own capital city as 0°, and the French continued to use the Paris Meridian until 1911.

The Royal Observatory in Greenwich was set up to try to solve by astronomy the problem of calculating longitude at sea but in the end the answer lay in being able to know the time at a given place, known as the Prime Meridian. For British sailors that place was Greenwich, and by comparing local midday with midday in Greenwich they could work out how far east or west they were; the problem was in making a timepiece accurate enough to tell the correct time after months at sea, a seemingly impossible task in the 18th century. John Harrison made that task his life's work and eventually succeeded in designing the *H4* chronometer which lost only 15 seconds after 156 days at sea. Greenwich Mean Time, and the use of the Greenwich Meridian, have since become international standards and are still used for navigation even in an age of atomic clocks and Global Positioning Satellites.

For landlubbers in the 18th century, knowing the exact time was of no great importance. In the days of horse-drawn coaches local time in Plymouth was 20 minutes ahead of London because of its distance east, which was a trifling insignificance after a 22-hour coach journey but which became important with the arrival of the railways, whose operators needed to synchronize their train times. The main east-west lines used Greenwich Mean Time from their opening in 1838–41 and the other railway companies gradually followed suit until the country was unified as one time zone, known colloquially as Railway Time and, later, as London Time.

As time came to be more important to people the number of public clocks began to grow, some of the most prominent being at railway stations. This one holding up the traffic in Peckham was commissioned by the London, Brighton & South Coast Railway in 1860 and graced Victoria Station for over a hundred years before being exported to America in 1971. The Peckham firm of Evan Cook crated the clock for Robert Freeman and shipped it to San Francisco, where it was hung in his themed restaurant, which was called… Victoria Station.

The flying statues pictured here are one of a series by Guy Portelli, sculpted for the revamped London Pavilion, and the 13-ton South Bank Lion, 150 years older, being lowered into place at the eastern end of Westminster Bridge. The original London Pavilion was a 'song-and-supper room' attached to the *Black Horse Inn*, and became a music hall in 1861. A new London Pavilion was built in 1885 whose façade still stands, with the addition, in 1987, of Portelli's sculptures. The building became a theatre in 1918, a cinema in 1934, and closed in 1982; it was restored in 1987 and the top two floors are now home to Piccadilly's Rock Circus, a collection of wax models of rock legends.

The South Bank Lion is also known as the Coade Stone Lion after the woman who invented the material from which it is made. For this is no ordinary stone lion but a piece of remarkably resilient pottery, fired in a kiln and showing no signs of age after more than a century and a half. Artificial stone has been manufactured since Roman times but Eleanor Coade's carefully guarded formula created the most weatherproof stone ever made, which was used for statues and decoration on a number of London buildings including the Norwegian Embassy, the National Gallery, the Royal Opera House and Buckingham Palace.

In 1769 Eleanor Coade set up her 'Lithodipyra Manufactury' on the site of the present Royal Festival Hall, taking over a factory previously owned by Richard Holt and, after the lapse of his patent, improving on the artificial stone that was made there. The factory closed in 1840 and the secret formula was lost but during the 1970s the British Museum Research Laboratory worked out the composition of the stone: it is also known that the process involved firing the mix twice for days at a time at temperaures high enough to almost liquefy the stone. The name Lithodipyra was the only clue Eleanor Coade gave away as to her secret formula, being a composite of the Greek words for stone, twice, and fire.

The lion was originally red and stood above the entrance arch of the Lion Brewery near Hungerford Bridge, where it made a memorable impression on French novelist Emile Zola – after a visit to London in 1893 he wrote, 'it amused me greatly, this British Lion waiting to wish me good morning'. The lion survived the Second World War, when the Lion Brewery was blitzed, and was moved to Westminster Bridge in 1951 as part of the Festival of Britain celebrations. After the Festival of Britain it was moved to the entrance of Waterloo Station at the request of George VI but returned to its present home in 1966, a particularly apt spot being roughly on the site of a gallery opened by Eleanor Coade in 1799 to display over 1,000 examples of Coade stone.

above

Holborn tram station in the Kingsway tunnel, closed soon after this photograph was taken and later reopened to road traffic as the Strand underpass. 1st April 1952.

A vast amount of 'secret London' is hidden away below ground, including a six-acre subterranean government office complex beneath the Treasury, disused Undergound stations and tunnels, wartime deep-level shelters now used for data storage, and Mail Rail, a miniature, driverless rail network used by the Post Office to deliver mail. There are also some 200 miles of cast iron pipes belonging to the erstwhile London Hydraulic Power Company (once used to supply power for lifting things like safety curtains in West End theatres), the underground cells of the former Clerkenwell House of Detention, and a three-storey electricity sub-station beneath Leicester Square, whose ventilation extract shaft forms part of the cut-price ticket booth in the corner of the square.

Two other features of underground London are the Kingsway tunnel and the Brompton catacombs. Holborn Tram Station, pictured above, may be a thing of the past but the Kingsway tunnel will be familiar to any drivers who have used the Strand underpass. Kingsway was opened by Edward VII in 1905 and named in his honour; other suggested names included Empire Avenue, Imperial Avenue and Connecticut Avenue. The new 100-foot wide road, built to relieve congestion on the narrow thoroughfares of Drury Lane and Chancery Lane, cost £5 million and included the novelty of a purpose-built tram subway from Theobald's Road to the Embankment. The subway was raised in height from

1929–31, closed in 1952, and the southern part opened as a road underpass in 1964.

The catacombs beneath the Brompton Cemetery are usually closed to the public but on 31st August 1995 they were opened to general view for European Arts Day. The catacombs are part of Benjamin Baud's unfulfilled design for the cemetery which, like Baud's payment, was a victim of the fact that the West of London and Westminster Cemetery Company ran out of money. Baud's design was for a wide main avenue leading to a large central Anglican chapel flanked by two smaller chapels for Roman Catholics and Dissenters, with long arms of catacombs forming a 'Great Circle' and extending for the full length of the cemetery beyond. The octagonal central chapel was built, as was the Great Circle which is now filled with tilting graves and memorials, but the smaller chapels were never built and the catacombs left uncompleted. The cemetery was consecrated in 1840 and sold to the General Board of Health in 1852, becoming the first cemetery to be run by the state.

Those laid to rest in the Brompton Cemetery include Frederick Leyland, whose extravagant tomb was designed by Edward Burne-Jones, Samuel Cunard, who founded the Cunard Steam Packet Company in 1840, the year the cemetery was opened, Henry Mears, founder of Chelsea F.C., and Samuel Sotheby, whose epitaph might have read: 'Going, going, gone...'

Another underground treasure is the vaulted, brick-lined Victorian reservoir beneath Wildcroft Road in Putney; above ground the reservoir is a cricket pitch. Like the Putney Heath reservoir, most of London's water network is underground, one notable exception being Thames Water's enormous manometer on the Shepherd's Bush roundabout. Not only is the manometer a measure of the mains water pressure but it is also a reminder of the remarkable feat of engineering that is hidden away below ground: the London Tunnel Ring Main is a 50-mile long tunnel, 130 feet below ground, big enough to drive a car through. Michael Caine hasn't yet repeated the driving skills he learned on *The Italian Job* but in 1993 ten cyclists rode through a one-and-a-half mile section of the tunnel as part of a charity bike race.

As well as building reservoirs to supply the people of London, the Victorians were also concerned with removing waste, and most of London's drains and sewers are the brainchild of one man: Sir Joseph Bazalgette, Chief Engineer to the Metropolitan Board of Works. Bazalgette's system, completed in 1875 at a cost of £6.5 million, is still in use today and comprises 1,300 miles of sewers on three levels; the upper two discharge by gravitation while the lowest level requires pumps. One of the glories of the entire system is the ornate Abbey Mills Pumping Station near Stratford, affectionately known as 'The Cathedral of Sewage'. It was built by Bazalgette and Edwin Cooper from 1865–68 as one of four main pumping stations and it is still in use today, although it has since been converted to run on electricity rather than steam.

London's need for a practicable sewage system was just as great as the need for a clean water supply. As long ago as 1290 the monks of Whitefriars petitioned Parliament that the 'stinking ditch'

right
The restored Victorian reservoir under the cricket pitch at Wildcroft Road, Putney.
1st May 1992.

of the Fleet River, which was used as an open sewer, had caused the deaths of several brethren, and, in a lesser-known extract from his *Diary*, Samuel Pepys writes that 'going down into my cellar… I put my foot on a great heap of finds… by which I find that Mr Turner's house of office is full and comes into my cellar, which doth trouble me'. What little sewage was carried away from people's homes by the open sewers was simply flushed into the Thames, the main source of London's drinking water supply, resulting in frequent outbreaks of cholera.

During the long, hot summer of 1858, known as the 'Great Stink', the stench from the river became so bad that sheets soaked in chloride of lime were hung over the windows of the Houses of Parliament and Prime Minister Benjamin Disraeli described the Thames as 'a Stygian pool reeking with ineffable and unbearable horror'. That same year a bill for the purification of the Thames was passed and the following year Bazalgette set to work on the capital's first properly planned main drainage system, with the Abbey Mills Pumping Station as the *pièce de resistance*.

'Oranges and lemons, say the bells of St Clement's…' It's a well-enough known couplet but it seems that nothing in life is that simple – the church whose peal is known to so many, and which gives out oranges and lemons to local schoolchildren, is apparently not the one in the nursery rhyme. The first clue is that the bells of all the churches referred to in the nursery rhyme have such similar rhythms, and that is because the nursery rhyme does not copy the sound of the bells but the other way round: the 10 bells at St Clement Danes that famously peal 'oranges and lemons' to the traditional tune were not hung until 1957, creating a dubious link with the original nursery rhyme.

St Clement was the Bishop of Rome, who was martyred by being thrown into the sea with an anchor round his neck. Several churches bear his name, and it is thought that the church referred to in the nursery rhyme is probably St Clement's, Eastcheap, which stands near the wharves where at one time citrus fruit from the Mediterranean was unloaded. Sir Christopher Wren rebuilt the church from 1683–87 after the Great Fire, at a cost of £4,365 3s 4d, and the parishioners were so pleased with the result that they sent Wren a third of a hogshead of wine.

St Clement Danes survived the Great Fire but was pronounced unsafe in 1679 and, apart from the tower, was entirely rebuilt by Wren. The church was bombed in 1941, when the interior was gutted and most of the bells cracked; the cost of rebuilding was met by the RAF and the Commonwealth and Allied air forces, and it is now the central church of the RAF. The new peal of bells was cast at the Whitechapel Bell Foundry where the original bells had been cast in the 16th century. The event was attended by the High Commissioner for Australia, who asked that a brass emblem be placed in the church in honour of the 5,000 personnel of the RAAF who lost their lives on active service in the UK.

The church holds an annual 'oranges and lemons' service, after which schoolchildren from St Clement Danes Primary School are given an orange and a lemon; the service is said to symbolise 'the old connections between the Wren church and the landing of fruit at the Thames Street wharves at the foot of London Bridge', a statement which only reinforces the claim of St Clements, Eastcheap, being so much closer to London Bridge.

above

Sir Thomas White,
High Commissioner for
Australia, attends the
re-casting of the bells of
St Clement Danes at the
Whitechapel Bell
Foundry. 5th May 1955.

Until it was demolished in 1934 the most curious 'riverside des res' in London was this pepper-pot toll-house, part of the original Chelsea Suspension Bridge – the upper part of the house, from where the tolls were collected, faces onto the roadway of the bridge. Chelsea Bridge was freed from tolls in 1879 and the toll-house later became home to the May family, seen here relaxing in their garden at the corner of Battersea Park.

The first bridge on the site was designed by Thomas Page and built from 1851–58. Only five years after this photograph was taken it was replaced by the present bridge, designed by Rendell, Palmer and Tritton. The railway bridge in the background is in fact a pair of twin bridges, known in the 1920s as Victoria Bridge and built five years apart for two separate railway companies both serving Victoria Station. The double bridge was rebuilt by Freeman Fox and Partners from 1963–7, with the original piers being encased in concrete, and is now known as Grosvenor Bridge.

During the digging of the foundations of Chelsea Bridge, human bones and Roman and British weapons were found, showing that a battle must have been fought there, and it is thought that Battersea Marshes was the place where Julius Caesar crossed the river in the 7th century – without the benefit of a bridge.

While he was working on Chelsea Bridge, Thomas Page also designed the present Westminster Bridge, which was built from 1854–62 and replaced the one on which Wordsworth found inspiration for his poem *Lines Written Upon Westminster Bridge*. Charles Dickens the younger was not a fan of Page's architecture, calling Chelsea Bridge 'thin' and levelling the same criticism at the 'long, lanky piers' of Westminster Bridge; he did, however, concede that 'when the river is full, and the height of the structure reduced as much as possible, there is a certain grace about it'. Presumably, then, Dickens would have been happy to see a flood of the proportions mocked up by *The Sunday Times* in this picture of Westminster, a sentiment that would not have been shared by the May family.

below
David Fautley adds the
final pieces to Legoland's
version of Tower Bridge.
The Legoland theme park
opened in 1996 on the
old site of the Windsor
Safari Park.
3rd August 1995.

Dickens might have been more complimentary about Tower Bridge except that it wasn't built until 1894, six years after he was writing – and the final pieces of this version of the bridge were not put into place until more than a hundred years after that, in 1996, as part of the Legoland theme park in Windsor. Lego means play-well, a name coined by its inventor Ole Kirk Christiansen from the Danish words *leg godt*, and it is a phrase that could well be applied to the Tyburn nuns. Tyburn is more famous for its river, tree, and gruesome executions than for its convent but within ecclesiastical circles the nuns of the Tyburn Convent are well known for their sporting prowess, recently hosting the first Nuns' World Snooker Championship and organising a sponsored skip to raise money for urgent building repairs.

The ancient River Tyburn flowed from South Hampstead through what is now Regent's Park, where it was later borne over the canal by an aqueduct, and on to join the Thames at Westminster. It gave its name to Tyburn Road (now Oxford Street), Tyburn Lane (now Park Lane) and, most notoriously, to the Tyburn Tree, the gallows close to where Marble Arch now stands.

For more than five hundred years Tyburn was London's main execution site, until 1783 when the gruesome spectacle moved to Newgate Prison. The triple gibbet of the Tyburn Tree was capable of hanging up to twenty-one victims at a time, many of whom were executed for petty crimes, and in all nearly fifty thousand people lost their lives, amongst them 105 Catholics who were martyred during the Reformation.

The Tyburn Convent was set up in 1902 as a shrine to the Catholic martyrs, and it is the home of 25 sisters of the Adoration of the Sacred Heart of Jesus of Montmartre, who fulfill a commitment to pray continuously for the souls of the martyrs. The Tyburn nuns spend all their time in study and prayer apart from an hour a day when they are allowed to relax; snooker and Scrabble are their favourite indoor games and when the weather is good they go out into the convent garden to skip or play football, badminton, or netball. The nuns are members of an enclosed Benedictine order, which means that despite the prime position of the convent close to Marble Arch they must never leave the building, not even to visit relatives or go shopping on Oxford Street.

This book opened with three images of Nelson's Column and it ends with a close-up of Britain's maverick naval hero apparently having his ears waxed. But Nelson, now such a prominent London landmark, only really made his presence felt in the capital after he had been pickled in brandy for three months and put on display in the dining hall of the Royal Naval Hospital at Greenwich. Thirty-seven years later, in 1843, the 17-foot high Craigleith stone statue of Nelson was placed on its granite column, from where he has enjoyed magnificent views of London ever since.

An estimated 100,000 people came to see the statue on the ground before it was hoisted to the top of the 170-foot column, and it was said by the *Spectator* to have 'a daring disregard for personal resemblance'. However, sculptor E.H. Baily was proved right in exaggerating Nelson's features in a staute that would rarely be seen from closer than 170 feet.

Nelson was famous for disregarding orders, and the cleaning of his ears might have been ordered by the Royal Navy's senior admirals except that it was by ignoring Admiral Sir Hyde Parker's signal to disengage the enemy that Nelson won the Battle of Copenhagen. And in any case, the problem was not his hearing, it was his eyesight: as he put his telescope to his right eye, which he had lost while assisting the army ashore at Calvi, Nelson said, 'I have a right to be blind sometimes… I really do not see the signal.'

Copenhagen confirmed Nelson's place as a national hero, he already having won a knighthood for his courage and skill at the Battle of Cape St Vincent (where he lost his arm), and a baronetcy for destroying the French fleet at the Battle of the Nile. Superstar status was clearly a phenomenon as early as the beginning of the 19th century, for it is said that on leaving his Portsmouth hotel for the tour of duty that would culminate in the Battle of Trafalgar, Nelson had to use the back stairs to avoid the crowd that was waiting outside for a glimpse of the naval genius.

When news of the Battle of Trafalgar reached the Admiralty, just across the road from where Nelson's Column now stands, it was tainted with sadness: 'Sir, we have gained a great victory but we have lost Lord Nelson.' The battle took place in October 1805 but Nelson was not buried until January 1806; in the meantime his body was preserved in a barrel of brandy and brought to the Royal Naval Hospital in Greenwich, where he was laid in state for three days in the Painted Hall before being taken on his final journey up the Thames to St Paul's. No doubt he would not be amused by rumours nearly two hundred years later that the European Union had decreed that Trafalgar Square, along with Waterloo Station, be renamed so as not to offend the French.

right

Richard Paffett uses an air hose to clean Nelson's head. The statue is coated with an anti-pigeon gel to help stem the build-up of guano.
24th February 1987.

Index

A page number in *italics* indicates an illustration or the caption to an illustration. Individual streets, buildings, landmarks, etc are indexed separately from the areas of London where they are situated.

Acknowledgements

**The author would like to thank the
following people and organisations
for their assistance:**

Tony Bell, *The Times* Picture Library
Will Eaton
Marie-Claire Walton
The London Fire Brigade
Crisis
Peter Osgood, Chelsea Yacht & Boat Company
Axa UK
Iain Sinclair
Roy Porter
Rob Humphreys

Bibliography

Age Exchange. *Living Through The Blitz*. London:
Age Exchange, 1991.

Barker, Felix and Peter Jackson. *London: 2000 Years
of a City and its People*. London: Papermac, 1983.

Clout, Hugh (ed). *The* Times *London History Atlas*.
London: Times Books, 1991.

Dickens, Charles. *Dickens's Dictionary of London*.
Devon: Old House Books, 1993.

Duncan, Andrew. *Secret London*. London: New
Holland Publishers Ltd, 1998.

Hawkes, Jason. *Over London*. London:
HarperCollins*Illustrated*, 2000.

Humphreys, Rob. *London: The Rough Guide*.
London: Rough Guides, 1999.

Jack, Ian (ed). *London: The Lives of the City*.
London: Granta, 1999.

McAuley, Ian. *Guide to Ethnic London*. London:
Immel Publishing Ltd, 1993.

Porter, Roy. *London: A Social History*. London:
Penguin, 2000.

Simmons, Jack and Gordon Biddle (eds). *The
Oxford Companion to British Railway History*.
Oxford: OUP, 1997.

Sinclair, Iain. *Lights Out for the Territory*. London:
Granta, 1998.

Weinreb, Ben and Christopher Hibbert (eds). *The
London Encyclopaedia*. London: Papermac,
1993.

Wessex, Edward. *Royal London*. London:
HarperCollins*Illustrated*, 2001.

This edition produced for
The Book People Ltd, Hall Wood Avenue,
Haydock, St Helens W A I I 9UL

First published in 2001 by Times Books,
HarperCollins*Publishers*
77-85 Fulham Palace Road
London W6 8JB.

Compilation copyright © HarperCollins*Publishers* 2001.

The Times is a registered trade mark of Times Newspapers
Limited, a subsidiary of News International plc.

Layout Designer: Colin Brown

Indexer: Susan Bosanko

Picture credits/ copyright © 2001
All photographs copyright © Times Newspapers Ltd with the
following exceptions:

Andrew Stenning 43; Associated Press 65 top, 74 top, 143;
Central Press Photos 144, 146, 147; Geraint Lewis 59, 117
bottom, 207; Hulton Getty 2, 52, 92, 112, 113, 115, 128, 132, 135,
136, 145; James Morgan 189; Jo Reid & John Peck 31;
Kemsley Picture Service 36, 41; Keystone 102, 137;
Liffe Holdings Plc 126; Mark Pepper 24 bottom; Planet News
74 top, 83, 86, 192; Press Association 178, 202; QA Photos Ltd
22; Rex Features 21; Universal Pictorial Press & Agency Ltd
13, 24 top, 154 right.

The publishers have made every effort to trace copyright
holders.

A catalogue record for this book is available
from the British Library.

ISBN 0 00 765007 8

Colour origination by Colourscan, Singapore

Printed and bound in Spain